MW00873487

THE CALL TO
AFRICA

THE CALL TO
AFRICA
ONE WOMAN'S JOURNEY
TO SERVE GOD IN AFRICA

GLENDA OWENS

XULON PRESS

Xulon Press
2301 Lucien Way #415
Maitland, FL 32751
407.339.4217
www.xulonpress.com

Unless otherwise indicated, Scripture quotations taken from the King
James Version (KJV) – *public domain.*

Scripture quotations taken from the Holy Bible, New International
Version (NIV). Copyright © 1973, 1978, 1984, 2011 by Biblica, Inc.™.
Used by permission. All rights reserved.

Printed in the United States of America.

Paperback ISBN-13: 978-1-6312-9549-2
Dust Jacket ISBN-13: 978-1-6312-9550-8
E-Book ISBN-13: 978-1-6312-9551-5

TABLE OF CONTENTS

DEDICATION

This book is written and dedicated in memory of my sister, Joyce E. Owens, who lived out a lifelong dream and calling to serve God in Africa. And also to the memory of her co-worker, Maxine L. Gordon, who had already served in Africa for approximately eighteen years before being teamed up with Joyce. They both had a very deep desire to serve the Lord among the African people. Their lives were filled with many, many stories of excitement, persecutions, sickness, evacuations, and other difficult situations. Thanks to all her letters that I had saved over the years, I was able to compile this book and not just rely on my memory. Most of the script is in her own words as I copied from her letters. There were many, many more stories and photos that could not be contained within one book.

Special thanks to one of my nephews, Carl Owens Jr., who, along with his mom, Gale, encouraged me to write a book and offered to help. He helped me sort through all those letters, putting them in date order and making notes of special things to highlight. He also helped with graphic design of covers, scanning and adjusting photos, social media, e-mails and creating video clips for YouTube. Watch for these links scattered throughout the book.

The main purpose of this book is to show how God uses a life that is totally committed to serving Him, no matter the cost.

PREFACE

Listen!! What do you hear? Out of the deepest part of Africa come the sounds of—everything from chimps squealing in the forest to sounds of men chopping trees in the distance, or the sounds of drums calling, or gunfire. Could the gunfire be the Africans hunting for meat, or could it be from invading armies? Actually, it's both, at different times. But then at other times, life in the remote 'bush' can be very quiet, cut off from the city noises of traffic, sirens, etc. Something of intrigue seems to be calling. Just as a seaman 'hears' the sea calling to him, this is a true story of how Africa seemed to be calling a young girl. She listened to that 'inner voice' calling and saying, "Go ye into all the world," and she followed that call all the way to the heart of Africa, never regretting one moment of it, even though times would get very rough and challenging, with many detours and life-threatening situations. It has been said that once you've been to Africa, there is something that seems to call you back. Having been there myself, I agree.

Chapter 1

PREVIEW OF A DREAM

"Open that suitcase!"—the stark reality of being in Africa. The airport guards want to see what you have that they think looks interesting so that they can put a high duty on it or talk you out of it. One of the items that catches their eye is a bright orange outdoor extension cord, even though they have no way of using it. Or perhaps they would notice an extra baseball cap, and they reason that you only need one so they could use the extra one.

After hours and hours of bartering with officials and filling out endless forms in a hot little one-room shack, they would give the okay to load the little Cessna mission plane that had been brought out of its hangar out at the airport. But by this time, it might be too late to make the flight down into the 'bush.' Weather could change quickly after crossing the mountain ridge. So we would have to lock the loaded plane in the mission's private hangar and go back into town and stay overnight at the mission base until the next morning and try again. Although it is just around the lake, the road is so bad that it might take a couple hours or more one way. So you have to start out early.

The next morning is a mad scramble to get off and running to the airport again. Prior to loading the plane, everything has to be carefully weighed, and then the next morning, we would weigh ourselves again. Better not eat too much for breakfast.

Finally, we get loaded onto the little plane, and I mean loaded—sometimes to the ceiling with things such as a foam mattress or a basket with a chicken in it. Such is life in Africa. We taxi down the runway and quickly lift off. It's a small airport with only one runway. The scenery is grassy hills with animals roaming loose and little huts with people building fires to cook on. It quickly changes to dense forest.

As we fly over the rainforest, it looks like miles and miles of the tops of broccoli, and you wonder what it's like under that huge green canopy. Flying in a small Cessna plane, you are able to see for miles in every direction. The only break in the treetops is a river or a small village now and then. Everything is lush green, and fruit grows abundantly. Joyce just keeps saying, "I can't believe I'm finally in Africa." How could something so beautiful have so many difficulties? But she doesn't care because she is just so glad to finally be there.

After crossing the mountain ridge, the pilot points out a high cliff protruding out of the forest like the Rock of Gibraltar, and he says, "That is Ikozi," which means rock. Little does Joyce know at the time that it will eventually become her home for a while.

After flying over vast areas of treetops for about forty-five minutes, the pilot begins lowering his altitude and starts looking for the clearing in the forest that is the little airstrip. Finally, he spots it and circles to make sure it is safe to land—not too wet, nor any animals grazing on it. The Africans have been instructed to keep it clear, but that is not necessarily the case.

As the little plane taxies down the bumpy clearing, you can see many people who have come out of the forest to see what the plane

Preview of flying over jungle and Ikozi Rock, her future home.

is bringing in. They have heard the plane coming and have hurried to the airstrip. Their ears are trained to hear sounds before we can hear them. They are always alert to the various sounds of the forest, and they have gotten the word that some new people are coming.

As Joyce gets out of the plane, she looks all around at the sights and sounds of many people who have come to greet them, and again she says, "I can't believe I'm really in Africa!" It had been a very long journey, not just from America to Africa, but also a long journey in life to get to this point. What all goes into preparing for such a journey? And how many interruptions and detours? It definitely is a test of perseverance and endurance.

Chapter 2

PREPARATION FOR A JOURNEY

Every journey has a beginning, no matter how many twists and turns; and just like a river, it carves a path as it goes along, leaving indelible marks along its path. Our lives are like rivers that wind their way through many places and situations and eventually empty into an ocean whose shores touch around the world.

Joyce's journey began in July 1939 in Galveston, Texas, where her family lived at the time. Galveston is an island in south Texas and had the only hospital in the area at that time. Joyce was the second-born child of what would eventually be five, following a brother named Carl. It was told by one of our aunts that when Mom held the newborn Joyce in her arms, she said, "This baby will be different." Little did she know just how different life's path would take her.

Two years later, I was born (the third child), and shortly after, the family moved inland from Galveston to the small town of Hitchcock, where eventually two more children were born, Kenny in 1944 and Carol Sue in 1949. Hitchcock is fifteen miles by road from Galveston but only a few miles (as the crow flies) from the bay. It was a small farming community built along the railroad, so produce was shipped north by rail. It was also home to the largest blimp base, which was built during World War II to house blimps that would 'guard' the Gulf coast from any enemy invasions. The blimp base was also part of the military base known as Camp Wallace, which housed many personnel during the war. We often would run outside our home to watch the blimp go over. We only lived about a mile or two from it.

Times were very hard during and after the war. Money was 'tight' and some commodities such as sugar were rationed. Dad held several jobs, trying to support the family, one job being a truck driver for a propane delivery service as well as other companies. We moved from one rent property to another. One time, we even shared a large two-story house with another family. Dad also worked off and on for the railroad, eventually working there as a switchman until his retirement many years later. We didn't see him through the week because he worked the night shift and would still be asleep when we left for school. We didn't dare make any noise while he was sleeping. Dad was of English descent and was very strict. We learned manners, respect, responsibilities, and obedience. He could whistle very well, and he had a loud shrill whistle when calling us. He expected us to be within calling distance, and we had better come as quickly as possible. We learned to listen for that whistle.

Those years of 'pinching pennies' were not easy, but they were part of the preparation process for the years ahead. As kids, we were taught to pitch in and help with the chores. Mom worked hard keeping up with five children, washing clothes outside on a scrubboard, and cooking meals from 'scratch.' She would always raise a small garden with vegetables. And she also raised chickens, so we had plenty of eggs and perhaps a chicken for Sunday dinner. We had running water but no hot water or bathroom facilities. We hated to have to go to the 'outhouse' at night with a flashlight because we had to share it with daddy-long-legs spiders and sometimes a snake.

Being on the Gulf coast, Hitchcock had an ample supply of heat, humidity, rain, mud, and varmints such as snakes, spiders, mosquitoes, roaches, etc. Since we didn't have air-conditioning, it could be pretty uncomfortable, especially at night. In those days, it was usually safe to sleep with the doors and windows open to let in any breeze there might be. But then that also let in the mosquitoes, and we would have to try to sleep with the smell of "Flit," as Dad was determined to chase down every mosquito with the spray gun. Living on the coast, we were also prone to hurricanes. We usually had to seek shelter elsewhere because we figured our little house was not strong enough to withstand a powerful storm like that.

We lived right next to the bayou which emptied into Galveston Bay. When we weren't playing in the water, we could also be found in the 'woods' behind the house. It was an old pear orchard that had been abandoned, and the weeds and undergrowth had taken over. We spent hours and hours climbing trees and carving out trails, yet always listening for that shrill whistle of Dad calling us. It also became a hiding place for us. This would also prove to be a means of preparation for Joyce's days of having to hide in the jungles of Africa many years later.

Joyce had a strong liking for the outdoors and was a tomboy, always trying to find a reason to be outside. She would always say, "I have an idea," and we would say "Oh, no," because her ideas usually meant that someone would get hurt. For instance, one of her ideas was to build a board ramp up over two sawhorses and have us ride our bicycles over it. She was the daredevil, but I didn't go for that idea. But years later, some of her ideas would prove to be very beneficial for others, as she was able to create projects to help the living conditions for the people in the forest of Africa. Joyce was used to doing without some things, so she could 'make do' in almost any situation.

Joyce also had a love for horses, and one of our neighbors across the bayou gave her an old horse that she named Brownie. It wasn't much good for anything except bucking her off, but she was determined to ride and would just get back on. Joyce would build a fire at night so it would keep the mosquitoes off of him. One night, Brownie hovered over the smoke until the rope on his harness weakened from the heat, and he discovered he was free. Of all the places for him to go, he of course chose the well-manicured lawn of the well-to-do businessman who lived across the road from us.

Joyce & siblings & Grandpa with her beloved horse.

Another incident with the horse was when Joyce tied him to an old pear tree in the yard. The tree looked like it was half dead, but it always had a lot of pears on it. This particular day, Brownie decided it would make a good scratching post for his rear end. As he scratched, the old tree shook, and pears began dropping on him. The more pears that fell, the more he bucked and jumped. We all had a good laugh.

Being a tomboy, Joyce struggled in school. She often felt that she didn't fit in with her classmates and just wanted to be out riding her horse. She always longed for adventure. One day, she and I and a friend, Gale (who later became our sister-in-law), found a fox in the woods behind our house. This was right down Joyce's alley—lots of excitement.

Although we didn't have a lot of material things, our Mom was a quiet person with a strong faith in God. She always made sure we were in Sunday school and church services, even if it meant walking to church because we didn't always have a car. She had a strong influence on us and wanted all of us to grow up with knowledge of the Bible. When Joyce was only twelve years old, she asked Mom about something the pastor had said about what it meant to be "saved." Mom explained that she needed to surrender her heart to the Lord and serve Him. Joyce vowed to do just that, and right then, she dedicated her life to the Lord, quoting the Bible verse John 1:12 as her reference: "But as many as received Him, to them gave He power to become the sons of God, even to them that believe on His Name" (KJV).

We attended a small Bible church not far from where we lived. We often had visiting missionaries from various countries describing their work on the field, complete with photos and sometimes slides and curios of faraway places in the world. One Sunday, we had a visiting missionary from Africa, and Joyce was totally fascinated. She later told her family, "I'm going to go to Africa and be a missionary." We all laughed and said, "Joyce, you don't have any money, and we're too poor. How do you think you can go to Africa?" But Joyce didn't let the teasing deter her. God had planted the seed through that visiting missionary, and a call to Africa tugged at her heart. At age sixteen, she surrendered her whole life to serving the Lord and said she wanted to go to places where people had less opportunities than we did.

As time went on, friends of the family, church members, and many others learned of Joyce's persistent goal of becoming a missionary to Africa. For the small-town residents of Hitchcock, Africa seemed like a distant, exotic world away, and Joyce's dream seemed unattainable. But the pastor learned of her ambitions and encouraged her to go to a Christian camp during the summer. Dad said no at first because we didn't have the money, but Joyce was determined and raised the money doing yard work. Some from the church also helped financially. The pastor also suggested that she then go to get her training at a Bible college after high school graduation. This would be the first leg of the long journey to Africa.

Chapter 3

THE JOURNEY BEGINS

Pack your bags—time to leave for camp. Attending summer camp was the beginning of a taste of life away from home. And yet, in some ways, it was much like home—small cabins in the woods with no air conditioning but plenty of heat, spiders, and snakes. Dad had to drive her over one hundred miles each way, and back then the trip took all day because there were no super-highways. You better be sure to use the bathroom before starting the trip because Dad didn't want to stop along the way.

Joyce had always wanted to leave Hitchcock because she didn't feel that it had what she wanted. At this Christian camp, she met a whole different group of teens who knew how to have fun without getting into trouble. And it was so far out in the piney woods of east Texas, you could yell and scream and sing at the top of your voice without being heard in town. The games and activities they played were rough-and-tumble, just like Joyce. She met lots of new friends, many of whom had interests like her to go into Christian service of some kind. In fact, one girl told her about Dallas Bible Institute, where she was going to be attending. Attending a Christian camp is such a life-changing experience. She didn't want to leave camp and go back home, where she knew there was no life like that for her, but that's what she had to do.

After returning home from camp, it was time to settle into the doldrums of looking for work after high school graduation. There were miscellaneous jobs of babysitting, yard work, and helping around the house. Finally, she got hired at an insurance company in Galveston as a file clerk and typist. All the while, she was saving money to be able to go to Bible college someday to get whatever training she could that would prepare her for the mission field. She never knew what was in store for the rest of her journey, but she never gave up on her dream.

In 1957, after camp and her eighteenth birthday, she applied for acceptance to Dallas Bible Institute in Dallas, TX, and was accepted. She made the big move to Dallas and began her first year in the fall of 1957. It was a big adjustment, not like just going to camp for a week. And again, she had to start job-hunting. Like Moses in Exodus 4:10-12, she gave excuses of not being capable of the task; after all, high school had been a big enough challenge. And now college?

Joyce at Bible College.

Once she settled in to college life, she immediately made some friends—a few more tomboys just like her. They were always playing pranks on one another. But they didn't realize that their new friendship was about to be challenged by separation.

Temporary detour! Like all journeys, things don't always go as planned. In 1958, just as Joyce was beginning her second year at college, our mom was diagnosed with cancer. Our pastor wrote to her at college and advised that she should drop out of college for a while and come home to help the family. I was still in school, as were our younger brother and sister, so I couldn't help much. Her world came crashing down! How could this be happening? To be so close to fulfilling your dream, and yet this seemed like the end of the road.

It was so hard to say goodbye to all her friends and teachers at college, not knowing when or if she would ever return. But they all agreed to faithfully support Joyce in prayer for her and her family, and they assured her that this was the proper thing to do. As hard as it was for Joyce, it was also hard for Mom because she wanted Joyce to stay in college and fulfill her dream. It was always Mom who encouraged Joyce and told her to faithfully pursue her desire to serve.

Times were very rough, once again, as we all had to adjust. Mom was always the one caring for us; now it was our turn to help out and care for her. She eventually recuperated from that surgery and was back on her feet, but three or four months later, had to have more surgery. But this time, she was told there was no more cancer. So Joyce resumed her journey and headed back to Dallas to restart her second year of college in 1959. Once again, she had to start looking for a job. Dad didn't make a huge salary, so he couldn't afford to send her much money. She was basically on her own. She worked at the college to help pay expenses until she was able to find another job.

THE CALL TO AFRICA

As she resumed her studies for her second year of college, she was thrilled to be reunited with friends and to meet some new ones. One of those friends, Doris Lupold, was like a carbon copy of Joyce, and they became lifelong friends. They had nicknames for each other—Joyce called her "Loopie," and Loopie called Joyce "Hitchie" because of her hometown of Hitchcock. Those names would stick for life.

Those two, along with a couple other girls, became the pranksters of college. One instance was when they chased another girl with a cockroach. Even though that girl was the biggest of tomboys, she was deathly afraid of cockroaches, and she climbed out the window of the second-story dorm room and onto the roof to get away from them. They managed to get back into their rooms before anyone caught them. This was only one of many pranks that they would concoct to have some fun times while at the same time buckling down to study.

There were also times of trying to be serious and learn as much as possible. Joyce had taken piano lessons earlier in life, and so she wanted to continue that in college. She wanted to work somehow with music in her mission work, and she realized she needed more training. Her music teacher was extremely talented and expected Joyce to listen carefully and follow what she taught. Oh, the importance of listening. Joyce joined the choir and was able to make trips out of state to sing in various churches. This kindled her love for music.

By this time, her burden had increased for going to a foreign land, especially Africa. She saw the need of taking the good news of the Gospel to lands that didn't have the opportunities that we have. She had read in Romans 10:12-15 that there is no difference in people's needs around the world—all need to hear, but how can they hear? Beginning in verse 12 of Romans chapter 10, it says:

For there is no difference between the Jew and the
Greek; for the same Lord over all is rich unto all that
call upon Him. For whosoever shall call upon the
name of the Lord, shall be saved. How then shall
they call on him in whom they have not believed?
And how shall they believe in him of whom they
have not heard? And how shall they hear without a
preacher? And how shall they preach, except they
be sent? As it is written, How beautiful are the feet
of them that preach the gospel of peace, and bring
glad tidings of good things. (KJV)

This was pretty clear to Joyce, and her burden to go just increased
more and more. Someone needed to go, and she knew that she
needed to do her part.

During her senior year of college, she had been introduced to a
missionary who was home on furlough with Berean Mission of St.
Louis, MO. He gave her some literature on the mission, and she
began corresponding with them. She sent in her application and
waited to be notified. She was ready for the next leg of the journey,
no matter how long it would take.

She went on to finish college in 1962, but always joked that it took
her five years to do a four-year program because of having to drop
out for a year. She was thankful for the years at Dallas Bible Institute
and for the foundation that she felt was laid. She remained in Dallas
after graduation to continue working, but it wasn't always easy. Yes,
there were times of discouragement—being alone in a big city
and so far from home and family. She once started to pack to go
home, but then decided that it would make the Devil happy, so
she unpacked.

Chapter 4

DEVASTATING DETOUR

Once again, a change of plans. Joyce had to leave her job in Dallas and head home again. In early 1963, Mom was diagnosed once again with cancer—more serious this time. She endured several surgeries and many rounds of x-ray and cobalt treatments that were used. These treatments made her very sick and left her very weak. She progressively got worse, and on May 3, 1963, she was called Home and was now free of pain and hardships. Mom's death was devastating to our family because we were so close to her. She was the one who had worked so hard taking care of us, even while she was so sick with cancer. And now, at only age forty-eight, she was taken from us to her final rest. What now? Who would encourage Joyce? She had wanted Mom to live to see her go to the mission field.

Things seemed to unravel after Mom's death. She died about a week before Mother's Day, so it was especially devastating for us to see others celebrating with their mothers. Even though we knew Mom was in Heaven because of her faith in Jesus Christ, it was still very painful for us to be without her. We wanted everything to just stop and stand still, but time marches on, and life continues.

Our youngest brother, Kenny, was to graduate from high school in a couple weeks and receive an award for running track. Mom wasn't going to be there to see it. Another tough moment. And then our youngest sister, Sue (who was only thirteen), had to have a tonsillectomy. After coming home from the hospital, she woke us up to the sight of blood all over her pillow. Oh, no! What should we do? Where's Mom to help us? The doctor discovered that it was nothing serious, probably just a broken blood vessel or something. We had been saying, "What else can go wrong?" but after that, we learned to quit saying that, because something else could go wrong.

About a year or so after Mom's death, Dad remarried, and we were devastated again. We felt that it was too soon for him to 'forget' Mom. But as time went on, we found that she (Mary) was the perfect companion for him. She was a widow who had raised nine children, and she loved to garden, just like Mom did. She was an excellent cook and would cook vegetables from her garden. She, like Dad, never had the opportunity to travel while raising a family, so now they were able to start travelling. Since Dad had worked for the railroad, he could get a pass to travel on Amtrak for a reduced amount. They later bought a small travel trailer and would set out to places they had never seen before.

Both of our brothers joined the Navy, and our younger sister went to live with an aunt and uncle. I had just started a new job, so Joyce felt that she was not needed any longer to help with family matters at home. It was time for her to continue her quest to fulfill her dream. She went back to her job in Dallas to raise money for the next leg of her journey.

Chapter 5

THE JOURNEY RESUMES

Travel again? Not long after returning to Dallas, Joyce was able to make a trip through several states with a couple other ladies from the church to attend a Christian camp and eventually to the head-quarters of Berean Mission in St. Louis, where she had applied for acceptance. From there, she went on to Nebraska, where the mission held their camp, and while there, she learned that she had been accepted by the mission to go to Africa as a missionary. WOW—major milestone! But wait! They had just received word that Congo borders were closed and missionaries were being evacuated due to the latest invasion. Now they weren't sure where they would be assigned—Tanganyika, or go to Belgium temporarily to study more French? In the meantime, there was the task of deputation—more travel to raise support from various churches and individuals who would promise to support her on the mission field. This would take a year or so, but she would meet many people who would become her faithful lifelong supporters. Joyce didn't tell anyone of the closing of the Congo borders; she had faith that when God closes one door, He opens another. She went ahead with making arrangements to one day get to Congo.

In mid-August 1964, it was time to go home again to pack up most of her belongings and prepare for the move to the mission headquarters in St. Louis, where she would live until time to leave for the field. Could this really finally be happening? While there, she would sign up for two different classes of French. She was told that French would be beneficial in almost any country, but teaching someone from Texas with a southern drawl would not be easy. Oh, no—school lessons again!

Enter Maxine! Having just arrived in the States from Congo before one of their many wars, Maxine Gordon was staying at the mission headquarters when Joyce arrived in St. Louis. Being single like Joyce, she had prayed for a co-worker to share her burden for Africa. Maxine was sixteen years older than Joyce and had that many more years of experience on the field (since 1947), so this proved very beneficial to Joyce. They would become like a mother/daughter relationship in some ways but like sisters in other ways. Maxine had two brothers but no sisters, so Joyce became like a sister to her. They immediately bonded—similar likes and dislikes. Maxine was also raised in a small town like Joyce, only in Kansas, not Texas. She knew what hard work was. Over the years, it would become almost synonymous to say, "Joyce and Maxine," as one word when referring to them. Our family would tell Maxine that she was our "adopted" sister.

One final trip home! In December of 1964, Joyce was asked to come home one more time. But this time, it was for her commissioning service at her home church. They would officially commission her to go into missionary service and vow to support her. She wrote to our former pastor (who had moved to Alabama), who was instrumental in guiding her to Bible college and mission work. She asked if he would be able to come to her commissioning service and take part in it. He willingly accepted. This meant a great deal to Joyce. This trip home would be combined with Christmas with the family before her departure to Africa.

Back to St. Louis from Texas! Time for serious packing. Everything had to be packed in barrels for the long journey overseas. How do you pack enough for four years? That's how long a term on the field was supposed to last. You learn how to pack to utilize every bit of space. For instance, take some of the food items out of their boxes and put them in plastic bags and seal them tightly. And you also stuff whatever you can into shoes or any other 'cavity.' Space and weight are of extreme importance, as is distribution of weight; you don't want too many heavy items in any one suitcase. One little hint in packing is to separate a pair of shoes, putting each shoe in a separate suitcase or container. It's safer, and there's less chance of them taking the items when your baggage is searched at customs. They have no use for one shoe. And don't forget to list everything you pack into those barrels and boxes. The list must be typed and six copies made.

Besides all the packing, there had to be passports and visas obtained, which could take some time. And then there were medical clearances needed, which included lots of shots. Different countries each have their own requirements, and these shots have to be included in your passport. You feel like a pin cushion after all those shots.

The departure date had been changed a few times due to the unsettled situation in Africa. This made it difficult to make airline reservations. And some items had to be sent by boat, so they had to make arrangements for someone to claim them when they arrived over there. After considering France or Belgium as possibilities to go to while waiting for Congo to open its borders again, an opportunity arose to go to Burundi, a small country on the east of Congo. A missionary couple living there and working with Child Evangelism Fellowship™ (CEF) invited Joyce and Maxine to come stay with them. They would be able to learn Swahili while getting familiar with CEF literature, which they hoped to use in teaching children whenever they got to Congo. God always has a reason for delays or closed doors in our life. Joyce was reminded of Psalm 18:30a that says, "As for God, His way is perfect…" She now saw the reason for the delay in getting to Congo—to have time to get acclimated and learn the language before jumping right in. After all, life in Africa is a <u>huge</u> adjustment. They say that the first year on the mission field is one of just making adjustments and getting used to things.

While waiting for final clearance to leave for Africa, word was being received from the missionaries who were already in Congo that things were really getting bad. They were being evacuated, and many of the Congolese nationals were hiding in the forest. After about four months, they made their way out of the forest telling stories of how God miraculously took care of them through sickness, hunger, and cold. One man told of having to build a house twenty times as he had to move from one hiding place to another. But in spite of their sufferings, they would sing praises to God for protecting them, and they sang from the depths of their hearts. Joyce and Maxine wondered how long it would take for the situation to settle down enough for them to eventually get to live there. Everyone else thought they were absolutely crazy for wanting to go to Congo. Even some of our relatives were against the idea of Joyce going to Africa. But she had read the Bible verse in Galatians 1:10, which says, "For do I now persuade men, or God? For if I still pleased men, I would not be a bondservant of Christ." So they moved ahead with plans, still hearing the call to Congo and trusting God to work out the details.

Time to leave US soil, finally! Oh, the excitement as the time drew closer and closer. All the paperwork must be checked again and again—passports, visas, shot records, airline tickets, and the number of pieces of baggage, each one properly labeled. The date was set for July 30, 1965. I had flown to St. Louis to accompany them to Chicago, where they and three other women missionaries were to leave from. Oh, how hard it was to say goodbye, not knowing what was ahead for them, and yet at the same time, there was so much excitement and anticipation. Psalm 121:8 (NIV) assured us

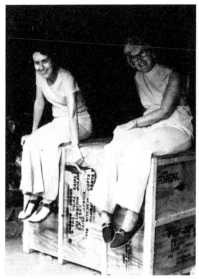 

Joyce and Maxine preparing to leave for Africa.

that, "The Lord will watch over your coming and going both now and forevermore." The road ahead would prove to be very eventful over the years, even life-threatening. But they were reminded of Psalm 139, verses 9b-10, which says, "… If I settle on the far side of the sea, even there your hand will lead me, and thy right hand shall hold me."

After leaving Chicago, they made a brief stop in Montreal, Canada (which just happened to be our dad's birthplace). From there, the long flight across the Atlantic Ocean took them to Copenhagen, Denmark, where they had a thirty-one-hour layover and time to visit a Danish church, which provided an interpreter for them to tell of their mission work. From Denmark, their next stops were Hamburg, Germany, and then Zurich, Switzerland. Next stop would be Athens, Greece, before entering Africa. Wow—halfway around the world in just a couple days. Finally, they would land in Bujumbura, Burundi—the tiny country on the eastern border of Congo, where they would be living for a year. On August 6, 1965, Joyce wrote her first letter from Africa to her family at home.

After the long trip, they were ready for some rest, but before they could get settled in, they were immediately informed that they were to catch the next flight out to Bukavu, Congo, to meet with other missionaries and church elders for some important meetings. This was to be a short trip, but after that long overseas journey, you are definitely not ready for more travel. However, this would be a fore-taste of life in Congo, where they hoped to eventually live.

This time, the plane was a much smaller two-engine prop plane. As the plane neared Bukavu in Congo, Joyce felt thrilled as she looked down to see many huts scattered over the rugged terrain below. She remembered what she had heard many years earlier from visiting missionaries, that there was a vast amount of territory to reach but so few missionaries. She remembered the words in John 4:35: "Look on the fields! They are ripe for harvest." She could hardly believe that she was viewing Africa for the first time and seeing the work that laid before them.

When the plane landed near Bukavu on the border of Congo and Rwanda, Joyce could hardly wait to begin that which she had waited so long for—working with the Africans. Her first letter home from Africa was bursting with excitement, which seemed to almost jump from the page. She wrote, "Well, I am now in Africa!! It is everything I had hoped it to be, only much more." As they drove into Bukavu, there were many Africans all along the road, and she soon learned that this wasn't anything unusual. Most of the people didn't own cars, so they walked everywhere. Many had bundles on their backs and heads which contained anything from straw to live chickens. When walking down the streets, the Africans are always approaching you to buy their curios and vegetables. You rarely ever pay the first price they offer because they like for you to bargain with them and settle on half the price first mentioned. In general, the Africans are very friendly and always want to greet you by shaking hands. Most of them have a good sense of humor, and you can't help but laugh with them at their expressions. And can they <u>stare</u> while they closely examine you!

Bukavu is built around a lake, lined with lots of trees and pretty flowers. There is evidence that at one time it was a beautiful city, before all the wars. It was said that at one time, it was called the "little Switzerland of Africa," however, most of the buildings are now riddled with bullet holes. There is also considerable poverty, but it is bustling with activity, even though the roads have been neglected and are in terrible condition. What cars there are in town are driven very fast over the pothole roads, and you better get out of their way because they may be trying to get some momentum going downhill before reaching the next hill.

After getting into town, the missionaries immediately went straight to the meetings they were scheduled to have. Having just completed so much travel, they were extremely tired. Joyce was having trouble staying awake, so they told her she could go take a nap, which she gladly accepted. You can't fight jet lag! After waking and putting on her tennis shoes, she kept feeling something odd in one shoe but tried to ignore it. After two hours, she decided to see what was making a tickling feeling on the side of her foot. She pulled off her shoe, and out came a nice-sized roach! Welcome to Congo!

Another comical incident came while trying to shop for groceries and supplies for the male missionaries who were planning to leave soon to go into the 'bush' to check on the mission stations there. While driving around town, they were stopped by the African police because they didn't have their Congo license yet. After the driver convinced him that the car was legally registered, he let them go, only to be stopped by another policeman. This time, he just wanted a ride. But after looking into the car, he saw that there was no room, so he just motioned them on. They don't mind asking. You can expect anything in Africa. If you own a small car, they will call it a "selfish car" because you can't pick up hitchhikers. If you own a truck or Land Rover or any vehicle with at least four seats, they expect every inch to be filled. Sometimes you wonder how the axle can hold all that weight. Although, that's probably why you see so many disabled vehicles beside the road.

Broken truck from overload.

After the two weeks of meetings while temporarily in Bukavu, Congo, it was time to return to Bujumbura, Burundi, where they would live until Congo settled enough for them to move there permanently. This time, they would make the trip by truck instead of by plane, since Burundi was such a small country right next to Congo. They rode with a missionary couple who had a double-cab truck, so there was plenty of room. This time, they didn't have to ride in a vehicle filled with people.

Now back in Bujumbura, the capital of Burundi, Joyce and Maxine would be living with another single lady in one room while waiting for their apartment to be fixed up. Besides fixing the inside, some screens and bars needed to be put on the windows, and the doors also needed iron bars to keep people from breaking in. For extra security, a night watchman was hired. Rent and other expenses were so high, there would eventually be four women sharing the expenses of the apartment. Now it was finally time to settle down into life in Africa.

Joyce and Maxine with roommates in Burundi, Africa.

Chapter 6

A NEW WAY OF LIFE

First, time to study again! After returning to Burundi, it was time to get serious about learning Swahili. Although many tribes have their own dialect, Swahili is spoken pretty widely. Joyce stated that she felt tongue-tied when trying to express something in another language. She also was able to resume her French lessons but thought Swahili was easier than French. The Lee family (who were the CEF™ directors for that area) would be their tutors in Swahili. Warren Lee kidded with Joyce and told her that she would have to teach a lesson in three weeks. Before long, she was excited to teach her first children's Sunday school lesson in Swahili. At one of their meetings, a teacher was standing at the door as the kids filed in, and one of them wiped his nose on the teacher's sleeve. The teacher just rubbed his sleeve on the next kid who came by.

The city of Bujumbura had a Christian radio station near their apartment, so they were able to have a children's program there too. Working at a radio station was a new experience. One particularly cute time arose when two little boys around four years old stood together holding hands and singing into the microphone. The children would line the road as they drove by, jumping up and down, shouting, "Hallelujah, hallelujah." They were so excited to have the missionaries coming to tell them stories. One Sunday, they had about 220 kids for the Sunday school lesson, and needless to say, they got pretty noisy. An African man walked into the little brick chapel with a handful of long grass about four feet long and tied together at one end. He took the grass and waved it around and around his head, and the rustle of the grass made the kids get really quiet. I guess they knew he meant business.

The days started getting busier and busier as more and more children's classes were added. This would give Joyce opportunities to hear and use Swahili. She liked it more every day and again commented how good it felt to be there.

Saturday mornings were for grocery shopping at the market, and what an experience! The open-air market had rows and rows of Africans selling anything from handkerchiefs to green beans. Most things were neatly arranged on the ground. But you definitely didn't want to buy meat at the open market—you go to a grocery shop for that. One thing that caught your eye was the pretty printed cloth they were selling. Lots of bright colors. They were used for everything from clothes to tablecloths to slipcovers for chairs. The material was durable and would last a long time.

Living in Burundi was quite different than Congo—no forests, but hilly streets lined with trees. The capital city, Bujumbura, was on the lake (like Bukavu, Congo), so the scenery was quite beautiful, with the Congo mountains in the distance on the other side of the lake. Joyce longed for the day when she would be living in those mountains. Their house was close enough to the lake to go have picnics there, even on Christmas Day. Being near the equator, there was not much change in seasons, but there was plenty of rain, and this would trigger Joyce's allergies. She always carried a box of Kleenex with her. Along with the tropical climate came lots of illnesses such as malaria, hepatitis, colds, etc., which caused a lot of downtime for the missionaries. Malaria was a constant battle, even though they took preventative medicine for it. It was like a bad case of the flu and would put you down in bed for a few days.

One day, the rains caused a large tree across the street from their house to fall. It fell right on the street, causing a roadblock. Soon a road crew came with their axes, working together in rhythm to a chant, got it cut up, and hauled it away for firewood. Another incident with a tree occurred when they tried to put up a clothesline and it pulled the whole tree down. Between the ground being wet and the tree roots having been eaten by white ants, there was nothing to hold the tree up.

Everything is different, including getting used to the water situation. Dry season brings haze in the air, which affects the water system. Even though you boil the water to purify it, it still looks brownish. One day, Joyce had to make a trip to the dentist, and he didn't have any water in his office, so he washed his hands in alcohol to clean them. The smell almost knocked Joyce out. And to complicate matters, he only spoke French, and Joyce didn't quite know enough yet. They had to call a third person to interpret. That could be pretty scary to have a dentist working in your mouth and you don't know what he is saying or doing.

And speaking of things being different, Joyce looked out the window one day and saw a dump truck going by loaded with men. They use them for taxis to take men to work. The men are packed in, all standing, and they are speeding along. The terrain is hilly, so they really get going fast going downhill. You also see lots of people riding bikes.

It became 'normal' to see soldiers driving around in Jeeps with guns, as once again, the political situation was unstable. One night, shots rang out within the block where they lived, so they all huddled on the floor in one bedroom and prayed. Even though there was a strong feeling of anti-American in town, they felt like God had brought them this far, and He would take care of them. Their Christian radio station was taken off the air for about three weeks, but later, was allowed back on. Mission transmitters were confiscated from several places. It seemed like this was going to be the end of their work, but once again, they were reminded of promises from the Bible. In Revelation 3:8, it assured them that "no one can shut the door that Jesus opens."

The opportunity arose to make a quick trip into Congo again to check on their visas and the barrels that had been sent on ahead. A small four-seater plane was made ready for their flight. How thrilling it was to be able to look out from that plane as far as the eye could see and view some of God's creation. While there in Bukavu, they were able to go to a place where they work with gorillas. You had to climb a ladder to the top of a barn and then walk out on a bridge over the gorillas. Maxine didn't want to climb a ladder, so the caretaker took her around to the gate for a look inside. An old pet donkey had followed them, and the minute they opened the gate, he went in. What a circus it was as they tried to get him out!

After that short trip to Bukavu, Congo, they returned to Bujumbura, Burundi, to continue the children's work. An opportunity came to start a new class that was about a thirty-minute drive from town. They would use a message drum to call the children to classes. On the way home, a driving rain came down, which made it even more dangerous. The road went around the side of a mountain with a drop-off cliff on the other side. The windshield had something sticky on it, so the wipers only smeared it, making it very difficult to see. But they felt like the trip was worth it—thirty children responded to the Gospel message. Classes were even held in a refugee camp where they would have 350-400 kids every day. Can you imagine trying to do craft time with that many kids? These kids didn't even know how to hold a crayon.

During another trip, the road was so bad that Maxine had to drive her little Volkswagen 'Bug' in second gear. They came upon a big hump in the road, and on the other side of the hump was a huge hole covering half the road. It looked deep and was filled with water. Maxine swung the car sharply to the left, and they barely missed having the whole front end of the car go down into the hole. Most of the roads over there are treacherous because they are constantly washed out from all the rain.

Maxine's VW stuck.

One day, there was a parade in town for their Independence Day, complete with a bunch of soldiers. One of the other missionary ladies had gone to help the school boys' class that was in the parade. Joyce and Maxine figured they would go take her a Coke before bringing her back home, knowing that she would be very hot and tired. Just as the soldiers marched in front of their car, there was a loud pop, and they thought it was a gunshot. But after checking, they found that the Coke in the car had 'blown its top' in the heat. The lid flew up and hit the ceiling of the car and then came down on someone's head. They all had a good laugh and were relieved that it wasn't a gunshot. But so much for a good cold drink.

The vehicles over there really take a beating from those roads. Most of them are four-wheel drive in order to negotiate the rough spots. One of the vehicles they drove to their meetings was a big old Volvo station wagon. Joyce was so short she had to use a pillow to be able to see over the steering wheel, but then she could barely reach the pedals. The window on the driver's side was missing, so in dry season, you got covered with dust. By the time all the workers plus Joyce and Maxine got in, there were eight people in all. One time, they came to a barrier in the road and had to stop. The soldier asked them to open the hood to search for arms. They couldn't find how to open it. Instead, they accidently turned on the windshield wipers. Even the soldiers had to laugh and motioned them to go on.

In April of 1966, Joyce and Maxine began making plans to finally move to Congo and out of Burundi. It would take months of preparation, but this was what they had waited for. They hoped to be moved by September, but it wasn't until October when they were able to get settled into the east African base for Berean Mission in Bukavu, Congo. Immediately, they were flooded with the need to have children's meetings. They were coming by the hundreds—hungry to hear the message of God's love for them. Was there really Someone who loved them? They were willing to sacrifice their playtime to stay and hear more. Once again, Joyce and Maxine were able to hold meetings in a Congolese refugee camp about an hour and a half away. It was obvious that these children had not been exposed to spiritual matters. Witchcraft was prevalent in most areas, and one of the barriers (checkpoints) they had to pass through to get to the meetings had a skull hanging on it.

Chapter 7

FINALLY IN CONGO— A DREAM FULFILLED

Shortly after moving into Congo, they had the opportunity to make a trip by road for a week down into the 'bush' for the first time with some other missionaries. There would be three carloads going, and it would be a very long and tiring trip, but Joyce was ecstatic because her dream was finally coming true—to meet the village people she had heard so much about and to see what 'jungle life' was like. Was this trip an eye-opener!

They left Bukavu at 9:00 p.m.—twelve people in three vehicles—on a dark, rainy night to begin their safari down to their stations in the bush. After two hours of slithering through mud, they discovered the fan belt missing on the pickup truck. They searched and searched for a spare, but found none and decided that the only option was to return to Bukavu in one of the other vehicles. By this time, it was 2:00 a.m., and the remainder of the group that had stayed shifted the loads in the other two vehicles and everyone was able to get some sleep, though not much.

The next morning, they were awakened early by the chatter of pedestrians and little boys tending their cattle nearby and wondering who these strangers were camping in the middle of the road.

They scrambled out of their vehicles and prepared what they could for breakfast while waiting for the others to return from Bukavu. By 10:15 that morning, the group in the pickup returned, and they were on their way again. They stopped for lunch by a rushing stream, and what a refreshing rest that was. After resting for a couple hours, they started out again, but they soon got separated. On the winding jungle 'roads,' it was hard to see if one of the vehicles got delayed for some reason. Sure enough, the pickup truck had problems with its front wheels.

Crossing a stream while stopping for lunch break.

They continued on after a bite to eat but soon got separated again. Those in the lead stopped by a village to wait for the others. Soon the villagers came out and invited them in to their village. They shifted the load again in their International Scout and were able to get some sleep. It had rained all night, and the others hadn't arrived yet, so they decided to visit with the Africans while they waited. When there was no sign of them by 7:00 the next morning, they decided to go back to see what had happened. Their gas was low, and the road was too narrow to turn around, so they started walking. It felt good to get out and walk. They found the others in the pickup truck, and after having so much trouble with it, they decided to leave it in a nearby village until someone could fix it. Some of the Africans are pretty good mechanics.

After twenty-six hours on the road, they had only gone thirty miles. The next morning, they continued on their journey, only to be stopped again. There was a big truck being repaired in the middle of the road with no room to pass. The big trucks are used by the mining companies (gold and diamond mines in the area), and that's what keeps the roads torn up. Since they couldn't get around it, that meant camping in the vehicles again for another night. The next morning, the men had to dig a path around the truck, and eventually they were on their way, only to get stuck in the mud later. They were wondering if they would ever get to their destination. Maxine had made that trip many times in the past, but she said this was the worst she had ever seen it. No wonder the cars and trucks just fall apart. They had to make many stops along the way and ran into a few other people trying to get their vehicles out of the mud. Sometimes the villagers would invite them in for a meal while they waited to continue their journey. It was a continual battle of getting the vehicles unstuck from mud, and sometimes even the Land Rover would almost turn over.

It took four days to get to their first station, Ikozi, and there were two more to get to before turning around and heading back to Bukavu, eventually. It had taken a week to go less than a hundred miles. Joyce wrote in one of her letters that she could never, never describe what those 'roads' were like. But the missionaries were always received with huge, warm welcomes from the Africans. At one point, they had to leave their vehicles on one side of the river and go across on a ferry. The people were all waiting for them on the other side, waving their arms and singing songs such as "Shall We Gather at the River" and "Anywhere with Jesus I Will Safely Go." It was the first time they had seen some of the missionaries since the last rebellion when all missionaries had been evacuated. They passed out tracts and even had children's meetings all along the way.

The people were always so eager to hear a Bible story and learn a new song. Were all those mud holes worth it? Joyce knew that Congo was definitely an open door for the Gospel. She was thrilled to be there and eager to get started.

She quickly got a taste of 'life in the bush' and was eating some things she had never eaten before. The main staple is rice, which is well irrigated, being in the rainforest. The Africans stake out their gardens on the side of a mountain and chop down what trees are needed to make room for the garden. The dead trees are allowed to dry before burning, and then they just plant the seeds among the remaining stumps. Being on the side of a mountain, it provides perfect irrigation. After the rice is harvested, the women pound it and then use their winnowing baskets to separate it from the chaff.

The men go hunting for such meat as monkeys, porcupines, birds, etc. Joyce mentioned that barbecued monkey tasted like beef. They have the type of palm trees that grow large clusters of nuts at the top, and the men go up a rope ladder to cut them down. It's a huge cluster of nuts, so look out below when it falls because they weigh a ton. The women pound the nuts and then when they cook them, a reddish oil comes out, and that's what they use to cook with. Chicken in palm oil is quite tasty and a main dish. There is a type of greens they can get from the forest that is seasoned with a hot pepper and is always served with rice. Being in the tropics, there is a wide variety of fruit such as pineapple, bananas, papaya, avocados, lemons as big as grapefruit, and rose apple which makes a delicious

Road hazards, ferry crossing, and Maxine teaching a class outdoors.

*Women separating palm nuts; clearing forest for rice gardens;
Joyce holding monkey given by hunters.*

apple pie. It looks like a combination of an apple and a pear and has the grainy texture of a pear.

After two and a half weeks of being down in the bush (it was supposed to have been only one week), it was time to return to Bukavu. But this time, the women would fly out in a small plane. This was Joyce's first time to view the Kivu rainforest from the air. She couldn't get over how beautiful it was. They would have liked to stay longer, but they had children's meetings scheduled in two different schools in town. The trip had taken longer than planned, so they were glad to make it back in time. They had 420 kids enrolled in one school. Each class lasted an hour and fifteen minutes each day. Can you imagine working with that many at a time? There were 222 that said they accepted the Lord as their Savior. Only God knows their hearts and whether they are sincere. They had an African worker with them who also had trained with them while in Burundi working with the CEF™ literature. Their literature is excellent for teaching children because they use lots of visual aids and songs. The people just begged for more each time they taught a lesson.

One Saturday, they decided to take a break, so they accepted an invitation from another mission that had just bought a huge plantation-like place, complete with a few race horses. This was music to Joyce's ears. She never thought she would be horseback riding in Africa. It was a beautiful place with rolling hills that looked like they were covered in green velvet. What a place to relax after what they had been through on that trip down into the bush.

Living in Bukavu could be a bit chilly at night in the rainy season, so having a fireplace felt good. The days would get extremely busy as they gathered supplies and made plans to move down country for good. They started sending some of their barrels every time a plane or truck went that way. Since they would be so cut off from any place to shop, they had to really think of what all they would need. They never knew how often the mission plane could make a trip down to their stations, so they had to stock up on the necessities. That meant plenty of batteries for flashlights, matches, and kerosene for their tabletop cooking stoves, since there was no electricity. Another 'must have' would be sleeping nets to put over their beds to keep out the mosquitoes and palm gnats. This would be quite a new experience for Joyce, so she was glad to have Maxine, who had already spent some years in Congo. Joyce was in need of a new pair of tennis shoes, so she wrote and asked me if I could send her a pair but reminded me to send one at a time—less likely to be stolen.

Chapter 8

LIFE IN THE BUSH

In January of 1967, they finally received permission from the American Consul there in Congo to move down into the 'bush.' Things don't move fast in Congo, and they had waited months for this. The Consul agreed to the move, since the missionaries had a vehicle and two-way radios to communicate with those in the city. They would move down to their stations in shifts—three would go to one station and five would go to another. Among these, there had to be a man on each station, otherwise they might not be allowed to stay. Although they flew in, some would still need to travel by truck to the other station. The 'road' was so bad, the truck sustained a broken axle.

In spite of all the difficulties, Joyce and Maxine were thrilled to finally be where they would call 'home'—Ikozi station, the high rock they had flown over before. It was a small village clearing in the forest—very mountainous and beautiful. There was a small mud-brick school, church, dispensary, and a few other buildings. The little house they were to live in was in much disrepair, since no one had been there for quite some time. The buildings were deserted outposts of the Congolese army and later rebel groups passing through. They were made of adobe brick with slate floors, but the doors and windows were falling off. Some of the Africans were good at carpentry and were able to help fix up things, including the screen door that was falling off the hinges. They were also good at making furniture out of wood from the forest that was tied together with vines. Their couch only cost $8.00. Another African was able to clean out what there was of a bathroom. What a filthy job that was. During the time when no one was living there, the monkeys and chimps had taken over the house.

The house had two bedrooms, one bath, a kitchen and dining area, and a hall. There was an upstairs that had three rooms, which would be used for storage. The bedrooms each faced some of the Africans' houses, a small valley, and a waterfall. Beyond that, the hills were covered with the massive jungle. Utilities? No electricity, so they had to use kerosene lanterns and kerosene refrigerators. Cooking was done on a wood stove, which also was used to keep a large pot of warm water, as well as a charcoal iron for ironing clothes. Running water? The designated water man took two buckets to the stream and then back to fill the barrels if rain hadn't been sufficient.

To us, it didn't sound so wonderful, but Joyce described it in one of her letters as being like a "hidden paradise." They could look out all around and on a clear evening see seven ranges of mountains while experiencing all of the beautiful sunsets. At an elevation of 3,300 feet, the nights were chilly. It was so peaceful to listen to the stillness, except for the Africans going about their duties or the monkeys squealing in the trees. And what an abundance of fruit. Joyce considered it a privilege to be in such a beautiful place, and she wondered why God had chosen to place her there. Other than the physical realm, there were numerous opportunities to teach the Lord's work, and that was why they were there.

One day, she and Maxine decided to take a walk. As they came to one village, the people all came out to meet them and show how glad they were to have them there.

House at Ikozi with bountiful fruit supply and beautiful sunsets.

Joyce crossing stream on way to village, and children that came to greet.

One old man came and gave them an egg as a gift. They have so little but are so willing to share what they do have. Some would even give a chicken, a small amount of rice, or some fruit. The one thing they don't want is to be called "stingy." As they walked along, they learned of more and more villages, some deep into the forest. They wanted to go to those remote villages, but the Africans advised them not to. Even a trained African can get lost in that dense forest.

A very special occasion came about when Joyce was able to witness an African baby being born. The woman named her baby after Joyce—not only using Joyce's first name, but also Joyce's African name, Walia na Beingi, which they had given her. What an honor for Joyce. The woman had just accepted the Lord as her Savior before the baby was born, so Joyce got to witness a spiritual birth as well as a physical one.

On another occasion while visiting a village, one of the missionaries had a dog which followed them, and what a fiasco that was as the dog took out chasing a goat. The Africans are very defensive when it comes to protecting one of their goats. The chase was on with everyone chasing the dog, which was chasing the goat. The dog and the goat each had a high price on their head. They all were running everywhere, around the huts, through the gardens, and even around the toilets out back. Later, they had to laugh at how funny it must have looked with everyone running and yelling and screaming at the dog. But if the dog would have killed the goat, the missionary would have had to pay for it.

Life in the bush can be very difficult, not just because of not having access to facilities, but also because of the sicknesses and ailments that attack the body. There was always malaria to deal with in spite of taking anti-malarial medicine. It could ravage the body very quickly. Joyce and Maxine received word that an African friend of theirs was very sick and eventually went into a coma. There is one type of malaria that is very dangerous because it enters the brain and can be fatal. The missionary nurse gave the woman a shot to bring her out of it.

With the roads being so bad, the body takes a beating being tossed around in a vehicle. At one bad spot in the road, they hit it so hard that Joyce hit her head on the ceiling and then bounced back down and hit her side on a metal bar on the side of the seat. Her side seemed to always bother her after that. Since she was of such small stature, diseases and maladies seemed to always attack her, however, she was determined to stay and often wondered if Satan was trying to discourage her.

The next station, Katshungu, was thirty miles from Ikozi, and they had a newly completed airstrip for the mission plane to land on. From there, they could fly out to Bukavu (180 miles to the east) for medical help, or even further northeast to Nairobi, Kenya, which had better hospitals. They could stock up on whatever supplies they needed while in town. Maxine needed to see a dentist, and Joyce needed a checkup to see why her side felt continuously sore. The nurse feared it could be appendicitis, but after a checkup, it was determined to be a sensitive intestine caused from a change of diet.

After their checkups, they flew back down into the bush and landed at Katshungu, where the new airstrip was. This was the first time for the plane to land with a full load. They bounced a few times and discovered how much more work needed to be done to level the strip. More trees needed to be cut down to lengthen it. Mission pilots are very well-trained to land on such surfaces, but they want it to be as smooth as possible.

Trouble in town! Early July brought news of 'rumblings' in Bukavu. Since it was on the eastern border of Congo, there were frequent volatile situations with neighboring Rwanda, Uganda, and Burundi. Ever since Congo won its independence from Belgium around 1960, there were growing pains. Mercenaries had taken over the city and raided and burned many buildings. All communication was stopped when the local State man asked those down in the bush to surrender their radios. They lost contact with the missionaries in Bukavu who had to leave, and they had to assume that they were okay, although the word was that many of their belongings stored there were lost. Those down in the bush felt safe—all was quiet there. Most of the Africans had fled to hide in the forest, just in case.

The son of one of the missionary nurses was the only male on their station, and he was due to leave for the States to go to college. His mom was going to leave with him and see him off, but they would need a soldier escort to get out. That meant that Joyce and Maxine couldn't stay at Ikozi by themselves without a man on the station. They would have to temporarily move to their next station, Katshungu (thirty miles away), to be with the other missionaries. Katshungu had an airstrip in case they needed to be evacuated, and its station was larger than Ikozi, with several buildings including one that was used as a hospital. They hated to leave so soon, and even though the Africans were also devastated, they had no choice.

At Katshungu, they moved into a small place behind the nurse's house. It was right up against the edge of the forest, and the monkeys often came up to investigate. Nothing could be left outside for fear of the monkeys carrying it off. One day, Joyce stooped down to stare at one of them, and he mimicked her actions, staring right back at her. With little sunlight getting into the small house, the African workers began a tough job clearing away a large cluster of bamboo for them, saving the larger poles to build a chicken coop. When they burned the remaining bamboo, it surprisingly sounded like fireworks.

A handful of Congolese soldiers set up camp, right there on the station, to 'protect' things. Their target practice sure did pierce the quietness of the forest. They even moved into one end of the hospital buildings, but they didn't cause any problems and were polite to the missionaries—with some even attending their church services.

Evacuation notice! Things suddenly changed when they received a telegram saying that they were to all be evacuated by plane. They quickly packed what they could, but the plane didn't show up. For three days, they kept watching and waiting. Finally, they heard the plane circling the station—in the pouring rain. Since it couldn't land in the rain, the pilot dropped a note saying, "We'll be back tomorrow," and they were to display a white sheet if it was okay to land. Sure enough, at 10:30 the next morning, they heard it circling again. They all packed into the Land Rover and hurried to the airstrip about three to four miles away. When they got there, they saw not one plane but three mission planes. They all had to split up because the planes could only hold about four people each. Each plane took off with its passengers, and they hoped they would all arrive at the same destination. Joyce was relieved when her plane landed and she saw that the others were already there. After refueling, the planes then took them quite a distance away to safety in Luluabourg, where they continued to wait for their permanent visas—it had already been sixteen months. They later received word that their mission base in Bukavu was one of the buildings that had been broken into and looted. Joyce feared that all the slides she had left there would be lost. Other things can be replaced, but pictures can't.

Three months later, things were settling down, and there was hope of returning to their station. A man where they had been staying, who was a purchaser of supplies, had big trucks coming and going through their area at times, and he offered to help get them back. They could take large supplies of things such as flour, sugar, medicines, kerosene, school supplies, literature, etc. So they borrowed a big one-ton truck and set out to gather supplies. They rode in the back of the truck in a wicker chair, after using the chair as a step to get up into the truck. They got a lot of stares and laughs as they rode around town. But they learned it would take seven to ten days to make the rough trip back home, so they decided to go by plane and let the supplies go by truck.

While they were gathering supplies at the market, Joyce noticed a woman sitting by her produce, eating something. Upon further notice, Joyce saw that the woman was eating live flying ants. The Africans regard them as a delicacy. Joyce pointed to one that was crawling away. The woman quickly grabbed it and ate it. She offered one to Joyce, but Joyce declined—at first. On a dare, she finally decided to try one. She chewed real fast and then swallowed, making a face the whole time. One older woman who was watching made the motion as if the ant was still flying around in her stomach. Joyce nodded yes. The African woman said that if she chewed it up good, there was nothing to worry about.

Joyce and the other missionaries finally received word that they could begin making their way closer to home. One by one, they would fly to Kindu, which was closer to their village. They wanted to get as close as possible and let their people know they were coming back. They had been gone several months. When it was Joyce's turn, they flew around for thirty-five minutes but had to turn back because of bad weather. The next day, they tried again and had a very smooth flight. She was glad to once again meet up with the other missionary ladies who had gone before her. Because they were on the move so much, it was difficult to get any mail to or from them. They were always asking for mail but resigned to the fact that it was what it was.

While waiting in Kindu to return home, one of the Africans took them riding in the truck to a village about thirty minutes away. When they saw all the kids there, they couldn't pass up the opportunity to have an outdoor children's meeting. Joyce taught them the verse from Romans 3:23, which says that all have sinned. But when she asked them if it meant white people too, they said no. Again, she told them it meant <u>everybody</u> has sinned. She asked if they thought that she had ever sinned, and one little boy responded, "We don't know"—in other words, how would he know?

Finally, the okay was given to return to their home village. On Dec. 20, 1967, they loaded up the big Methodist Mission truck (where they had been staying), along with their driver and pastor, and headed out on the last leg of the trip back to their village. They were so anxious to get back that when they came upon another vehicle stuck and blocking the road, the three ladies got out and walked the rest of the way—about two miles. They arrived at Katshungu after dark that evening and surprised everyone. The Africans were out back behind their houses, sitting around the fire, and heard someone coming up. At first, they didn't realize who it was in the dark, but after recognizing Joyce's voice, they jumped up and mobbed them with hugs and greetings. A football game couldn't have been any noisier. There were many tears of joy. It felt so good to be back among their people. They were back in time for Christmas!

Chapter 9

WORK CONTINUES

Now that they were back at Katshungu, one of the first things they needed to do was to go out and check on the airstrip to see if it was still okay for the plane to land when needed. As they walked the three to four miles to get there, villagers in between would come out and beg for meetings. They also needed to go check on their house and belongings that had been left at Ikozi—their first home after arriving in the bush. They had hurriedly left there to gather with the others at Katshungu for evacuation when the trouble began.

At first, they thought they would have to walk the thirty miles because the 'road' was so bad, but then decided that the Land Rover truck might be able to make it. They were so glad to get there and find that all their belongings were okay. The people were so thrilled to have them back. Although they desperately wanted to stay, it would have to be a short visit.

They spent one week there taking inventory of all the needs—everything from medicines, school supplies, and clothes to just being hungry for attention. Joyce and Maxine immediately set out having children's meetings at the school for the first hour of school each day. The people were so hungry to hear the Word of God taught and to learn of His love for them. Even a teacher came to them and

Crossing log bridges and visiting another village.

wanted to know more. They walked to other nearby villages, and everywhere they went, they held meetings. They began seeing the fruits of their labors as more and more people expressed a desire to put their faith in Christ.

Danger stalks! After getting back to Katshungu, they were told of a dangerous encounter that four of the Africans had with a leopard. The men had gone deep into the forest to set their traps for some fresh meat. They hurriedly built a little shack to sleep in. The first night there, they heard a noise of heavy sniffing, and when they peeked out, they saw a huge leopard about twenty to twenty-five feet away. They took turns guarding all night with their spears. The next day, they saw him again following them. When a leopard stalks like that, he's out for a kill. They were scared stiff and thankful to make it safely back home. They agreed that it was only God Who protected them.

There would be many other times when they would witness God's protection as they went from village to village, sometimes staying overnight in one. During one such trip, they had to cross a river on a 'ferry.' As the African chauffeur drove onto the ferry, the engine quit. They decided it needed to be pushed back off the ferry and up a steep hill. So push they did, in the midday heat! After working on the truck for a while, the chauffeur got it started by letting it roll downhill, but because of no brakes, he almost went overboard into the crocodile-infested river.

Having no brakes wasn't the only problem. After that, the old truck just quit again, so they decided to walk almost seventeen miles to their next place for meetings. They had several Africans help carry their things on their backs, and they covered about eight miles before stopping to spend the night in a village.

When roads are too bad, you walk.

They were always met with very inquisitive children and adults. Now they saw the reason for the truck breakdown. The people couldn't believe that the missionary ladies would walk all that way to come and bring them the Good News of the Bible.

By the time they were ready to head home, their chauffeur and mechanic had the truck running again and came to meet them. All okay now? Not hardly. They mistakenly put kerosene in the boiling radiator! They discovered it in time before causing a disaster! Such instances were not uncommon in Africa. They didn't quite understand the full innerworkings of vehicles.

Life was far from boring down in the bush, and there was always plenty that needed doing. After the men chop down trees with their machetes to make space for planting the rice, they went off hunting or building while the women spent long days either in the rice gardens or pounding the rice after harvest to separate it from the chaff. Aside from teaching children's classes, Joyce and Maxine began teaching the women and older girls how to read and sew, planning classes for convenience around the women's time spent working in the garden. Women would get paid for their hard work with items of clothing and would be so proud to own a bra that they sometimes wore it on the outside of their clothing to show it off.

Joyce and Maxine stayed extremely busy, as other villages were wanting them to come. Because of bad 'roads,' a lot of travel was done on foot. On one particular trip, they walked a total of sixty-three miles, stopping along the way at different villages! When they did get to go by truck, even a Land Rover would get bogged down in the mud. It had started to rain, and they hit a hard bump. After that, the driver couldn't control the truck as it slid along in the deep winding ruts, slamming everyone around inside and almost turning over. When they finally came to a stop, the truck was leaning so much that Maxine looked out from her side and saw the ground! They discovered that the steering had gone out. After trying to push it out of the rut in the pouring rain, they decided to go on foot to the next village for help. They didn't mind walking—it was safer.

On their return trip, they were able to hitch a ride part of the way with someone who had a big six-ton truck. But even a bigger truck is not necessarily safer. As it crossed a wooden bridge, they heard the boards on one side crack under the front wheels. And now, what about the rear wheels carrying the load? As the rear wheels crossed, they heard the boards finish cracking, but they made it across! When they got out and went back to look, there was nothing left of the top boards—only the big log they had rested on. No one could figure out how that truck made it across. Only God! Psalm 91:11 says, "For He shall give His angels charge over thee, to keep thee in all thy ways."

As the days passed by, the work increased. They saw the need for more and more meetings, including teaching the Africans to teach their own people. Joyce learned that she was the first full-time children's worker to come to Congo with their mission. The need was tremendous, and she wondered if she could do it. But she reminded herself that the Lord chose her and she just needed to be faithful in serving Him.

There also was a great need for a doctor on their station. They at least had a nurse, but there were times when she was limited as to what she could do. For instance, one night, a boy was brought to them with a severe head injury. A house had fallen on him, and the skin on his forehead was peeled back to reveal skull bone! The nurse did what she could, working for a couple of hours, cleaning and dressing the wound. The boy survived and was later running around. There also were lots of instances in maternity when the nurse would have to intervene in a birth. Sometimes the baby was already dead in the womb before the mother came for help, and the nurse would have to literally pull it out. Life was not easy for those people. The missionaries would help in whatever area they could as the people came to them with their needs.

Some days it seemed that the only thing they were hearing was bad news—one thing after another. Word was received that there had been a ferry that sank in Kindu and an African friend had drowned. Then another day, a man was brought in with a strangulated hernia. Since they didn't have a vehicle that was working to take him elsewhere, they had to just give him something to relax him and have his friends take him home. Oh, for a doctor!

The work load continued, with other villages requesting visits and meetings. This required lots of lesson preparations. And with no vehicle to depend on, it meant walking—unless, now and then, a big mining truck would pass through and offer them a ride. Those old trucks weren't in good shape either, but it beat walking through all that mud. One old truck they rode in didn't have a cover over the gear box, and it was extremely hot and noisy riding in the cab. Joyce had to hang her head out the window to get some air, other than diesel fumes. She looked over at Maxine, and all they could do was laugh at their predicament. Maxine was not one to complain.

Help on the way! Word was received by radio that another nurse would be coming down on the next plane. Betty, who had left to escort her son out to attend college, was now returning, along with her daughter, Judy, who was on summer break from school. Most missionary kids (MKs) were sent to Kenya in east Africa to a mission school, and they would visit their family when possible. It would be so good to see them again, but Maxine had to scramble to get ready to leave on the plane's return trip to Bukavu. She was planning to get her VW Bug that had been left there and then try to drive it down country so they could have some transportation on the station.

It was a mad scramble to hurriedly gather things and walk the three and a half miles out to the airstrip to meet the plane. When they got there, a large group of people were already waiting. An outgoing patient who needed medical help would also be transported on the plane. After about an hour, they heard the plane buzzing the station and then circling back to the airstrip. The little red-and-white plane stood out so pretty against the dark green tree-covered mountains as it came in for a landing. The people all cheered and cheered as it taxied to a stop, relieved because it had landed with a full load. They quickly unloaded the plane and then reloaded for its return trip to Bukavu with some passengers. After the plane took off, they divided up the load that had been dropped off and then started the walk back in to the station. Everybody had something to carry.

Everyone helps carry the load.

After getting back to the station, they did lots of talking, catching up on all the news since Betty had left. She brought back some good news that more help might be coming. Although one of her sons had just left for college, her oldest son had just finished college in the States and would be coming out to help, along with two families. Finally, it looked like they would be getting some much-needed help.

Chapter 10

GOOD NEWS, BAD NEWS

Like the old saying "one step forward, two steps back," there would always be problems. Maxine had arrived with her little VW that she was able to drive down country. It would prove very beneficial, as they soon had to make a trip to Lulingu. They were so glad that they didn't have to walk this time. The trip was to see the local officials regarding a problem in the schools. The subsidized teachers had gone on strike and were blaming the missionaries instead of the government for not paying them.

On the way back, a dear Christian family stopped them and invited them to eat a delicious meal with them—chicken cooked in palm oil served with rice. The location was a terribly congested housing area, and as they came out, one little boy picked up a handful of sand and threw it at Joyce. They weren't sure why he did it, except that maybe he was jealous because they didn't eat at his house. Kids will be kids!

As they continued toward home, it was after dark when they reached the ferry crossing. The people there wanted them to stay and eat with them, but Joyce and Maxine said they needed to go on. So the people brought some food to them to take along their way. They sat on the ferry eating fish and rice, with a beautiful moon shining on the river. Even with all the problems, they would remind themselves that they were there because that's where they felt the Lord had put them. They weren't there to be loved by people, but to tell the people how much God loved them. Once they know how much you care for them, you have pretty much won their trust.

Every now and then, they would take some time out to relax. A stream flowed down out of the mountains and formed a waterfall, which formed a nice pool for swimming. The water was ice cold and relaxing. They would pack a lunch and go for a picnic to cool off. It was just far enough up the road to be away from the hustle and bustle of the station. You had to climb down the mountainside to get to it, so it was partially hidden from the path, giving a little privacy. Even still, there was always a lot of gawking from passersby.

The picnics were nice, but Joyce would eventually need more rest. All the walking from village to village had taken a toll on her. The nurse advised her to go up on the next flight and get checked out by a doctor in town. It would be her first time out in more than eight months. The doctor told her that she wasn't blessed with a rugged body and that she needed to live within her limitations and curtail some of those trips on foot.

Now that Maxine had her VW down on the station, they hoped that it would help tremendously. And another missionary, Betty, was going to be getting a new Land Rover to bring down country. That would now give them two vehicles on the station. But getting it there would be another story—constant bouncing over the ruts and trying to avoid going over the cliff. Thankfully, Betty's son would be doing the driving this time.

Once they were back home, they continued making visits to neighboring villages. One particular visit proved to be quite different. They were told that there were two men involved in a witchcraft cult who wanted to give up their fetishes. They had accepted Christ as

Wooden carrier (kipoi) made to carry Joyce after illnesses.

their Savior and no longer wanted any part of their past ways. They were to have another meeting the next week to burn the fetishes. In the meantime, the missionaries took them home to prevent anyone else from using them. When they went back the next Sunday, there was a huge celebration with a feast of chicken in palm oil with rice. They were shown the new church that was being built by one of the men who had given up the witchcraft. That could be very dangerous for them because of the culture which had been handed down by their fathers and grandfathers. Still, many people at that gathering were willing to also give it up and place their faith in Christ.

They had originally said they would burn the fetishes, but then the villagers decided they were afraid to do it in their village, so instead, they would dump it all in the river. But before doing that, one of the men took off his leopards' teeth necklace and gave it to Joyce.

Leopards' teeth signified strength and fierceness in that cult, but because he knew it wouldn't burn, he wanted Joyce to take it back to America to show people how their lives had been changed.

At another village they visited, the little VW took a beating. There were kids lining both sides of the 'road,' with big rocks in the middle of the road. To avoid hitting the kids, Maxine tried to navigate the car over the rocks, but the little VW sustained a badly bent suspension rod. It was able to be fixed at a nearby mining station, which had a garage. They were able to go on to the village for their conference. While there, they were invited to eat at the pastor's house. There were always a lot of kids standing around. Joyce's stomach suddenly growled really loud, and the kids looked under the table thinking it was the dog! She explained that it was her stomach, and everyone just about split with laughter.

Different cultures have different ideas on what a church service is to be like. One church they were visiting had appointed four men to take up the offering—two men for the regular offering and two men for the love offering. The two for the love offering wore red shirts (which they called blood colored) to signify Christ's blood. The Africans didn't have much money for offerings, so instead, they would bring such items as firewood for cooking, or small amounts of rice, or whatever they could spare. But they shared what they had.

Never a dull moment! No two days were ever alike. Back at Katshungu, it seemed there was always some kind of turmoil. Having the hospital and maternity there, someone was always being brought in. And there were other activities going on such as taking laundry to the river to wash, women pounding rice, having someone mow the grass around the house, or the men working on one of the vehicles. The older children were responsible for watching the younger ones while the moms worked, so there was always a hungry baby crying somewhere.

While the mother works in the rice garden, the children also have duties such as babysitting and chopping firewood.

As if there wasn't enough going on, a group of men came for school inspections. This inspection was for the mission station to get government subsidy to pay the teachers so that the missionaries wouldn't have to pay them. They had to take the inspectors over to Ikozi station to inspect their school too. As they passed through one village, they were given a chicken as a gift. They tied its legs together and thought it would be okay in the back of the Land Rover. But when they made a stop and got out, so did the chicken. Its legs had come untied, and it flew out and headed into the woods. They were determined to not let that chicken get away, so there went three guys chasing one chicken, laughing the whole time. They were able to catch it before nightfall, when a torrential rain poured for twelve hours.

Chapter 11

VACATION AND RELIEF

Look out for that elephant! Because life was so hard in the bush, it was recommended that they take a break now and then and go elsewhere for a few days. Joyce, Maxine, and Lydia Frank flew out to Bukavu, where they met up with another missionary lady and then flew up north to another mission station which had medical facilities. They all needed checkups, including eye and dental work. From there, they took a mission plane to fly up to another station that was at an elevation of 7,000 feet or more. It was cold but beautiful with lots of flowers. While there, they stayed with a doctor and his wife who were such a blessing to them. Good thing they were with a doctor because Maxine fell while playing tennis and got a slight concussion. After a few hours, she seemed to recover.

The doctor invited them to go with him to Murchison Falls Park in Uganda to meet a friend of his. After they got there, everything was all booked up and they had no place to stay at the main lodge, but they were offered some other buildings about a mile away to stay in. The ladies stayed in one building and the men in another. There were no curtains and no bedding. No one got much sleep that night, especially the men, because one guy snored so loud. The bathroom was an outdoor toilet, and with animals roaming around, you went at your own risk. This was a vacation?!

Sure enough, during the night, they heard noises. In the moon-light, they could see two hippos quite close. Toward morning, Joyce heard heavy footsteps getting closer and closer. Right outside of the window was an elephant passing by. Later that day, they took a boat ride for about three and a half hours up the Nile River and saw lots of hippos, elephants, water buffalo, antelope, and lots of crocodiles.

Later that afternoon when they got back to the lodge, they were sit-ting on the patio, and an elephant came walking by just the other side of the small stone wall. One visitor there stepped over the wall to get a picture, in spite of being warned not to do so. Those are not tame animals and are not predictable. Sure enough, the sound of his camera startled the elephant, and it began to chase the man. They all scrambled to safety, and fortunately, the elephant gave up and went on his way.

Elephants roam the plains, and sometimes invade villages.

That evening, they were offered a ride by three Peace Corps workers to go see the famous giant Murchison Falls waterfalls from the top. Along the way, an elephant was blocking the road. The African driver raced the motor and blinked the lights to try to get it to move. In its own time, it finally moved, but then their vehicle motor died!

After many attempts to restart it, they got out to push, all the while keeping an eye out for the elephant. They finally made it to the top of the huge waterfall there in the park. WOW!!! What a sight to see one of God's many awesome creations with enormous amounts of water pouring over the top.

Time to head home! Vacations are nice but also tiring, due to the travel involved. And yet it was necessary for them to get out for checkups, shopping for supplies, etc. As soon as they got back, they had to take Maxine's VW to the mining station garage to be worked on. There were gold mines in the area, as well as diamond, copper, and tin ore mines, so they had mechanics on hand for their large trucks. Those big trucks kept the 'road' pretty well torn up, but once in a while, the missionaries depended on them for help.

Betty Lindquist's oldest son, Jim, who had come back out after finishing college, was a huge help on their station. He proceeded to get the brick press machine ready so they could make their own bricks to build a small building for their Bible School, as well as more housing. The Director from the mining station said he would be sending a good mason to help them build the brick kiln to burn the bricks. It would be a long process which included drying the bricks thoroughly. Sheets of tin would be brought in for roofing. The Africans would go to the forest and cut trees to be used for doors and windows and benches. Some of the buildings on the station had been built earlier when it was a Belgian military post, but they needed lots of repairs after years of neglect. Jim was overseeing the work, and he had his work cut out for him, as more families were coming and needed extra buildings to be built.

Besides Betty and Lydia, another nurse arrived to help. Evelyn N. arrived, along with her barrels from the States. Unloading the barrels was always like Christmas, with plenty to share with others. She had brought lots of plastic items—everything from utensils to bowls to drinking glasses that someone had donated. They all were glad

Brick-making process includes carrying bricks on heads or by truck.

to get the items, since they had lost many items when their place in Bukavu had been looted earlier. Evelyn also brought out her accordion and began teaching Joyce how to play it. This whet Joyce's appetite to teach music.

Company coming! In addition to the missionary families who would be moving there, they received word that three other men would be coming down for a CEF™ Teacher Training course. Due to the horrible road conditions, it could take anywhere from a day and a half to one week to make the 180-mile trip from Bukavu. They might have to contend with landslides, bridges out, car trouble, or getting stuck. For the Africans who would be attending from other villages, some would walk over one hundred miles.

To help accommodate all the people coming, they decided to build new benches. The process of 'shopping' for trees to make the benches was quite a fiasco. After chopping down the right size, they had to figure out how to get the logs up the hill where they needed the benches. As usual, it had been raining, and everything was pretty muddy. They decided to use the big old truck to assist in their efforts. However, the truck didn't have brakes, so on the way back down the hill, they would slow down as much as possible and then have someone run along beside and throw the logs in front of the wheels to stop it. Quite a jolt, and no seatbelts or airbags!

Sure enough, the guys who were coming for the seminar got within two miles of the station and couldn't get any further, due to heavy rains and flooding. So Jim had to go get them with the big old International truck, which had no lights and no brakes. Since it was nighttime, they all took lots of flashlights to navigate through the mud, and it looked like a big Christmas tree in the moonlight.

Life in the rainforest could be very unpredictable. One day, the Bashi tribe came passing through with their cattle, and one old cow was too tired to go on, so they butchered it right there on the station.

The missionaries all chipped in and bought a leg for fresh meat. It tasted a little funny, and they figured it wasn't butchered exactly right. But it was fresh meat, which they hadn't had for a while because the State post guys (military) said the Africans couldn't hunt while the female animals are expecting babies. Thievery was starting to get bad, so the State post guys stepped in to handle it. If the thieves tried to escape, their wives would be held captive until they were caught.

Time to move again! The little house that Joyce and Maxine were living in was too small and cramped, so it was agreed that they could move into one end of the hospital building. It wasn't a big or modern hospital like we are used to seeing. It was a long brick building with cement floors, a tin roof, and an unfinished interior with bats that took up residence in the rafters. But Joyce and Maxine were glad to have the extra space, so they began fixing it up. The nurse lived at the other end of the building where patients were seen. Two other missionary families would be coming soon to live there and help with the work, so there was much to do to fix up the houses they would be living in.

Living in the rainforest meant a constant battle of fighting the elements, like dampness. One 'culprit' was the white ants (termites) that ate anything that was wood. Besides the white ants, there were driver ants, which were fierce—they could take a piece of flesh out of you with their pincers and could literally eat chickens alive, right to the bone. They came in droves, and interestingly, there were no spiders, roaches, or any other bugs after they left. They had to be driven out with kerosene or diesel fuel poured around the doorways or wherever they were coming in. And don't forget to be on the lookout for snakes. One was even spotted in the outdoor toilet! You better look good before you go in.

The nurses had their hands full. Evelyn had to go over to Katanti station to deal with a smallpox outbreak. Lydia and Betty stayed at

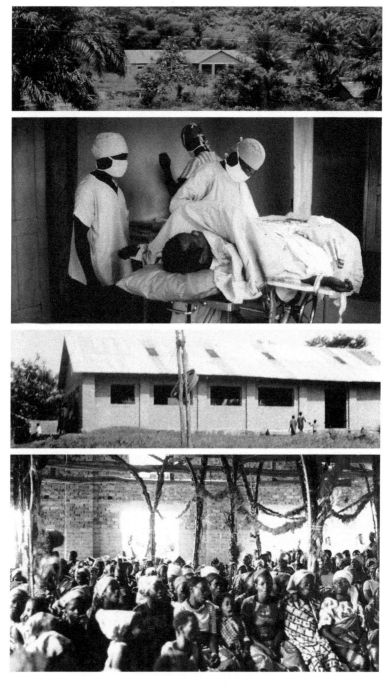

Hospital building in distance; surgery performed without electricity; church where everyone gathered.

Katshungu with Joyce and Maxine. Measles were also a problem, and the kids over there would get such severe cases. The nurses never knew what to expect. One day, a man was brought in from another village with a terrible wound that reached from his mouth almost to his ear. A tree had fallen and snapped a vine that whipped around and hit him in the face. It knocked some of his teeth out, and they were afraid that he had a broken jaw. So they loaded him into the big truck, and Jim drove him to Lulingu to see a doctor.

Never a dull moment! On one very hot day, they decided to eat outside and get some fresh air. Suddenly they heard a lot of noise, and they were told that a very large chimp was building his 'house' in a tree near Lydia's. A group of men decided to try to spear and trap him. They encircled the chimp, but it went right toward one of the guys who was afraid to spear it, and the chimp just leaped right over him and got away. They can be a nuisance, especially when they raid the pineapple patch.

Word was received that their mission headquarters had arranged to get a small plane for their area. Hallelujah! What relief! It was being sent to Nairobi, Kenya, in east Africa and then down to their area to be kept at the Bukavu airport. This would give them much better service, flying supplies in and out and being available for medical emergencies. The road was so bad that it was almost impassable by car or truck, and the missionaries were spread thin trying to cover all their stations. The Africans were thrilled too, because they figured that now maybe more missionaries would come. They all wanted their own missionary on each station, and they would ask, "How much does a missionary cost?" They wanted to buy one.

Chapter 12

FIRST FURLOUGH

Furlough—rest or work? Usually, a term on the field was supposed to be four years and then a year on furlough at home. But due to certain conditions on the field, it might get extended. Sure enough, it would be five years before Joyce and Maxine would get their furlough. The term "furlough" did not mean rest, by any means. They would have to pack up everything for storage while they were gone and arrange for the Africans to take care of it. And that meant writing up lesson plans for the Africans to teach classes during that time.

This furlough would take even more planning because they had invited me to come out for a month to visit, and then we all would travel back to the States together. They wanted to make a few stops along the way, like east Africa, Israel, and Switzerland, so this took months of planning and coordinating ahead of time because mail did not go through very quickly. After being in the 'bush' for so long, they were especially eager to spend a week in Switzerland resting and getting acclimated to 'civilization' again.

Besides all the long-range planning, they would have to get back to Bukavu to renew their passports and get other paperwork in order. This meant another trip over that horrible road. And horrible it was—even with a four-wheel drive vehicle. They were carrying cans of blackboard paint to leave at another station along the way, and after hitting a very bad bump, the paint went everywhere—all over the truck and the people. They started pulling weeds to mop it up. One of the Africans riding in the back bounced up so hard that he got a gash in his head from hitting the bar on the top of the vehicle. They put a temporary bandage on it until they could get to a doctor. All along the way, it was rain and hail and getting stuck time after time—five and a half hours in one spot and narrowly missing a landslide. They had to change a tire in deep muddy ruts and on an uphill slant. Just trying to go 180 miles to get to Bukavu was a major task.

Stuck again.

Finally in Bukavu, Joyce and Maxine would get as much done as they could before I would arrive on April 12, 1970. That same day, their new mission plane was being flown in to Bukavu after being inspected in Kinshasa, the capital of Congo. This would be the same plane that would take me down into the bush for the first time, and we would be its first passengers.

I arrived in Bukavu, but my suitcases didn't. They got lost somewhere along the way, with all the stops and changes of planes I had to make. And Joyce wasn't there to meet me as planned. Not knowing the language, I was about to panic until I discovered that another woman who had come in on the same plane spoke English and French, and she was able to interpret for me. They put me on the airport van to take me into town. Winding down the dirt road, we encountered another van coming from the opposite direction. As we slowed down to pass, I saw Joyce in the other van, and I started yelling, "Stop, stop!" We both got out and met right there on the side of the road. I was never so glad to see her—it had been five years since we had seen each other. Her driver had been delayed, and that was why she didn't make it to the airport in time. We spent the night in Bukavu before going on down country, and we hoped that my suitcases would arrive before we left. But that was not to happen. They didn't arrive until a few days later and had to be flown down on another flight.

My first flight down into the bush was beyond any expectation I could've had. Being in the little Cessna plane was so exciting—being able to see for miles in every direction. My head was swiveling from side to side, viewing the sights. The pilot started lowering his altitude long before I could spot the airstrip. And what a welcoming party there was when we landed on the little grassy airstrip surrounded by dense forest and mountains. Not only were they there to see a member of Joyce's family, but also to see the new airplane. They quickly began unloading the plane because the pilot's schedule was usually pretty tight—his turnaround time had to be quick in order to get out before the weather changed.

Mission plane with pod underneath for carrying extra baggage.

As we made our way the three and a half miles in to the station, I was amazed to actually be there, viewing the sights of another culture on the other side of the world. Most of their huts were made of mud and grass, with mud floors. Only a few of them were able to afford a tin roof. There was no electricity on the station—everything had to be run on batteries, and cooking was done on a wood stove. Water had to be boiled for drinking and cooking. Your drinking water was rationed, even for brushing your teeth. They greatly depended on rainwater, otherwise it meant sending workers to the river with buckets on their heads—their definition of running water. And since there was no running water in the house, you had to carry warm water by the bucketful from the woodstove in the kitchen to the bathroom. There was a bathtub with a drain, but no faucet. I had to adjust to a totally different lifestyle.

I was able to visit a couple of other stations while I was there and experience 'the road.' Not having my suitcases (they arrived right before I was to leave) meant that I had to borrow some clothes. Thankfully, Louise (daughter of a missionary couple) was about my size. And Joyce hurriedly made a dress for me from some beautiful cloth she had bought on a previous trip to Kampala, Uganda.

The scenery was beautiful down in the rainforest, and it was peaceful and quiet. At night, the moon and stars looked almost close enough to touch. Because there was no electricity at the time, they called 9:00 p.m. 'Congo midnight' because it was so dark. But I had a bad case of culture shock. I was anxious to get back to electricity and running water. And yet, as I said at the beginning, there is something about Africa that calls you back. Sure enough, over time, I was able to go back ten times—each time taking with me footlockers packed with supplies for them.

During my first visit there, I was kept busy not only with seeing the sights, but also helping them to get ready to return with me to the States. They even had me totaling grades for the Bible School report cards. There was a small Bible institute on their station, where men would come from other villages to attend. They would live there for four years, learning how to become pastors so they could return to their original village. Graduation day was always a very big celebration with a feast.

The day finally came for us to leave, and what a mad scramble. We had to load up everything in the truck and get out to the airstrip before the plane arrived. Joyce and Maxine had to make sure all arrangements had been made with the Africans who would be taking care of things while they were gone for a year.

Our first stop after leaving the bush was Bukavu, the mission center for their Congo work. There were many curio shops and sidewalk vendors, so I was able to buy souvenirs for those back home. Next stop was Nairobi, Kenya, where we not only visited other missionaries, but also visited a game park where we saw lots of different animals roaming out in their natural habitat. We took lots of pictures to show when we got back to the States.

Joyce feeding giraffe at Nairobi National Game Park.

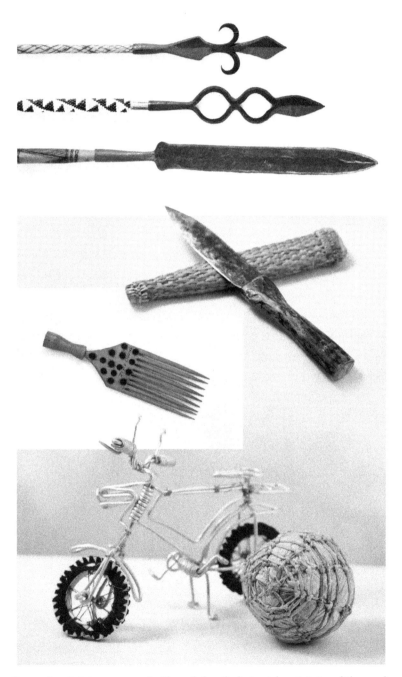

Souvenir miniature spears; knife and sheath; hair pick; miniature bike made from scrap wire and rubber; ball made from forest vine.

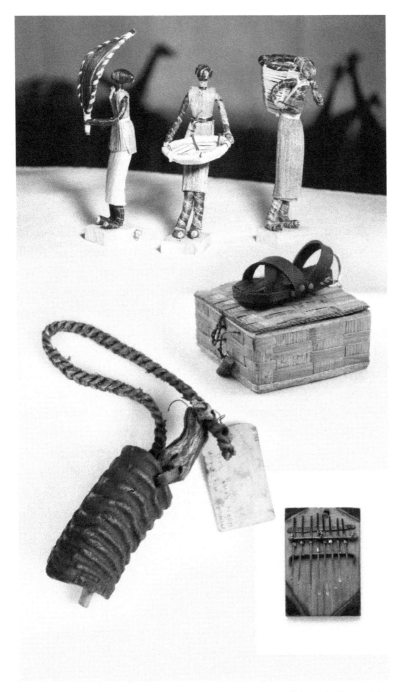

Miniature figures made from banana tree; miniature sandal made from old tires;
Masaii goat bell made from antelope horn; miniature hand harp.

After leaving Africa, our next stop was Tel Aviv, Israel, where we encountered a pretty thorough search going through customs. We had a limited time in Israel, but we did get a three-day guided tour. So much to see, and not enough time. But we did get to go down to the Dead Sea and wade in the water and taste it to see if it really was salty—we had to spit it out. It has so much salt in it, everything floats.

Next stop was Switzerland for a week of rest before hitting the States. We rented a car and drove up into the mountains. I was the only one among us whose driver's license had not expired, so I had to do all the driving. The car was a stick-shift, which I had not driven in a long time, and I was not experienced in mountain driving. What a ride! We laughed our heads off as we jerked our way up the mountains. But the scenery was so beautiful, it made the jerky ride bearable. So hard getting used to a clutch again! And trying to learn the different symbols on their road signs was another challenge. Once at our destination, we took a cable car ride up to the very top of the mountains. What a beautiful sight of the snow-covered Alps! And what a peaceful place to spend some time resting from all our travel before going on with more travel—Amsterdam, Holland, and then Montreal, Canada, before arriving in Houston. No rest yet—going through customs in Houston was worse than the search in Israel. Everything had to be taken out of our suitcases, and a price had to be listed for all of our purchases. Oh dear, why did I buy all those souvenirs, and how much were they?

Joyce and Maxine's time in the States would not always be a time of rest, as they began planning to travel around the States to all of their supporters, reporting on the work they had done the past five years on the field. Their travels would cover over 20,000 miles over the next few months, but it was worth it. After presenting their needs, churches and individuals provided such items as a chainsaw, a large bell for their church, a mimeograph machine (remember those?), Tupperware, linens, school bags, soccer balls, etc. They even raised money toward the purchase of a four-wheel drive International Scout with an electric winch on the front to pull them out of the mud. All of this, except the vehicle, had to be either packed in barrels or crated for overseas shipping. More work!

After a whirlwind year in the States, it was time to head back to where they now called "home" in Congo. They left in May 1971 from New York to Amsterdam, Holland. Once again, God provided a little 'extra' for them. The flight before theirs was a big KLM 747, which took most of the people that had been waiting, so their flight was half empty. And they were able to take all of their luggage without having to pay for extra baggage! There were lots of empty seats, so they could spread out and get some sleep.

While on their layover in Amsterdam, they were able to take a canal boat ride. And again, God protected them from harm when their boat had a narrow miss with a larger tug boat. They also enjoyed the fields of tulips—row after row of all different colors of tulips arranged in all kinds of patterns, as far as you could see.

Next stop would be Nairobi, Kenya, and again, they weren't charged extra for being overweight. After being met by a missionary couple (the Crumleys) who had driven up from Congo, they went to the freight area to claim their footlockers, which had been brought along as extra baggage. Maxine's was there waiting, and then Joyce's arrived while they were getting Maxine's. No extra charges had to be paid all the way from Houston to New York to Amsterdam to Nairobi. God is good!

They eventually made it 'home' to their station in Congo, and everyone was so glad to see them again. But soon they received word that the ship bringing their vehicle was finally due to arrive in Mombasa, Kenya, after being delayed. So they had to fly out to Kenya again and take a train from Nairobi to Mombasa on the east coast of Kenya. They were able to stay in a small cottage there that was owned by another mission. It was right on the Indian Ocean, and they could watch all the ships going by in the channel. They would collect shells while wading along the beaches.

There it is!!!! They got to see the actual ship coming in with their long-awaited vehicle on board. Since their cottage was right on the channel, they could read the large letters on the side of the ship— The Aimee Lykes from Galveston, TX. Here they were on the other side of the world, and to see something from Joyce's birthplace was quite exciting! Another missionary took them down to the docks two days later, and there sat their Scout! They were so relieved that it had finally arrived after its long journey. And it only had a slight scratch on one door and one flat tire. Not bad after such a long trip.

Now to look for one more barrel of goods that was shipped at the same time. The transport agent took them aboard the ship to look around. They met another man on board, and after talking with him, they discovered he knew someone that Joyce knew back home in Texas at our home church. The man was from New Orleans, but he knew Capt. Courtney, who used to go to our church and worked for that same shipping company. Small world!

After collecting their last barrel and the vehicle, they would start the long journey from Kenya back to Congo. Once they got to Bukavu, just inside Congo's eastern border, they would have to wait for all the paperwork to be cleared on it before driving it down country. Maxine and Joyce were both suffering from a cold and allergies, so they were ready for a rest before starting that arduous trip.

While there in Bukavu, they decided to have a wiener roast with other missionaries. It started raining, but they decided to endure and grabbed umbrellas, towels, or whatever else they could 'hide' under. Marge Crumley tipped her umbrella too much to one side, and all the rain poured off onto her husband's plate. They all had a good laugh, and the rain eventually stopped. In Africa, you learn to cope with whatever happens.

Chapter 13

BACK TO THE BUSH

Homeward bound! Clearance on the Scout to leave Kenya was finally received, so they quickly packed everything in it to head back to their station in the bush. After being gone for a year, they were anxious to get back, in spite of knowing what awaited them on that 'road.' The winch that had been mounted on the front of the Scout proved to be worth its weight in gold. It had to be used six times in just two days! The pilot's son went along with them on his motorbike. He would hold his legs straight out as he plowed through the mud, and then he would guide them through in the Scout. Everyone would be covered with mud, and by the end of the trip, they looked like they had been through a war zone.

Besides the mud, they would encounter other problems. While trying to pass through one village, the witchdoctors had set up a roadblock, threatening to kill anyone who tried to pass through while they were having their special rites. Joyce and Maxine decided to wait but later reported the incident to authorities because they had no right to block a roadway.

It was so good to finally be back home, but all the hard travel took a toll on them, especially Joyce. She kept experiencing pain in her abdomen, so the nurse insisted that she go to the doctor over at the

New Scout gets initiated on road down country.

Getting through one way or another.

mining station. He put her on some pills for amoebic dysentery and continued running more tests. Meanwhile, she lost quite a bit of weight, which she couldn't afford to lose. When the pain persisted, she decided to fly up to the Baptist Mission doctor and get checked further. He told her that the amoeba parasites had gone into the intestinal walls and into the liver, which meant taking a lot more medicines. He also said that once it gets into the liver, you never get rid of it, just control it with medicine. This was very discouraging news for Joyce, but she was determined to go on. The medicine caused some calcifications in the liver, and every time she had x-rays after that, it would show up as spots and would alarm doctors. She would have to explain that it was from medicine for parasites. Little did we know at the time that this was the beginning of a long ordeal for her and would later lead to something much more serious.

In spite of the discouraging news, they were eager to get back to the station and their work once again—Joyce teaching children's classes and Maxine mostly working in translation.

Joyce would type up courses in children's work to give to one of the Bible School teachers so he could help teach. She also had some artistic ability and would draw pictures to use in teaching the lessons. Sitting at her desk for too long would aggravate the liver problem, and her side would start hurting. The medicine helped with the pain, but she still had a problem trying to gain weight. Maxine would encourage Joyce to eat more so she could gain some of her weight back. Maxine would tell her, "Food causes swelling." Explaining her own weight, Maxine would say that there was a bounce on every ounce. She would never reveal her weight, even when having to weigh before getting on the little mission plane. She would just say, "I and my baggage weigh…"

Always on the 'backburner' was the desire to move back to Ikozi, where they first lived, but now with Joyce's medical problem, that

Joyce teaching and Maxine working with helper on translation.

would be pretty isolated from any help if needed. But they went ahead with plans, hoping to be there by Christmas, and sure enough, they made it. Once again, they packed up all their belongings, discovering how quickly you can accumulate things. The trip was utterly exhausting—nine hours to go only thirty miles! Another missionary accompanied them in his truck, carrying such items as barrels, furniture, and a fridge. As expected, they were constantly pulling each other out of the mud.

But it was so good to be home, and the people were so glad to have them back. It was just in time for a huge Christmas conference at their church, with all the school kids participating. They had a large response from the people, in spite of the fact that there was one dissident who was causing problems among the believers. He had been spreading lies, rumors, and accusations so much that the church had put him out. At one time, he had been the legal representative for the church. Sometimes the power of the position becomes too much to handle, and one can be bribed or 'bought.' Being the only two missionaries at Ikozi was often very stressful, with no one else to help with the work or in making decisions.

Cleanup time! After the Christmas conference, it was time for major cleanup. The house had been empty for a while, so there was much to do. The pilot's son, Bob, came over on a tractor pulling a trailer and was a great help—everything from painting walls and repairing the leaky chimney to cleaning the upstairs for storage. There was enough dust up there to start a dust storm. While he was there, he and some of the African men discovered a spot that could be cleared for an airstrip. That would be wonderful if Ikozi could have its own airstrip and not have to go over that horrible road to the airstrip at their next station, Katshungu. As it was, the pilot would have to just fly over and make a drop of mail or whatever food had been ordered over their radio, such as fresh vegetables or meat. One package of hamburger missed its mark and couldn't be found in time before the driver ants got a hold of it. They joked that it was 'ground beef' for sure! Another package got lost too, and in an effort to find it, they first cut down a lot of brush and trees. With the package still missing, they decided to burn off the area. The fire stopped within twenty feet of the package—a car part undamaged. Praise the Lord for airdrops in the forest and the fire stopping just in time!

Word came over their radio that the rest of the shipment of barrels had been cleared through customs and that they would be driven down to Katshungu in the new truck that had been purchased for airfield work. They were eager to get their barrels—although some items would be brought down on the plane such as the chainsaw and the light plant. That meant they would have to make another trip over the 'road' to go get them. So off they went—Bob driving the tractor and Joyce riding behind on the trailer, sitting on a trunk. One of the Africans wanted to send some of his goats to sell along the way too, but Joyce said no way was she going to ride thirty miles with goats. After collecting all their barrels and other items, they started back to Ikozi on the tractor, which ended up getting stuck, pulling the loaded trailer, and Joyce riding with the 'stuff.' She said it was so rough, it was like riding a bucking horse.

Electricity! After unpacking everything, they were able to get the light plant hooked up and have electricity in their little house. It looked so nice now, having been cleaned and painted. And on chilly nights, they had the fireplace, which had been cleaned and repaired. They were so thankful for their "little corner of the world."

Snake!!! Joyce woke up one morning coughing, and something caught her eye. As she glanced over to a footlocker beside her bed, she saw a big, long, black snake crawling over the top and then to the other side of the room. With one leap, she was out of bed and calling to Maxine. Because Joyce was hoarse from coughing, she couldn't yell for the Africans to come help. They finally got the attention of the men, and they came with machetes and a shovel. They tracked it down after it went into a closet and whacked its head off with the machete. It was a forty-four-inch-long deadly cobra! Joyce was so glad she woke up in time to see it before it disappeared. They were reminded of Psalm 91 that tells of God's protection.

Joyce again had to be flown up north to see a doctor after having persistent pain. The doctor said that in addition to the liver damage from parasites, she also had colitis (inflamed colon). She would really have to watch what she ate, and with medication, it could be controlled. It was hard enough adjusting to another kind of food, but now having to 'watch' what she ate was even harder. There was plenty of fruit in their area, but even too much pineapple could be irritating to a sensitive digestive system. One good thing they had was papaya, and that is supposed to be very good for digestion. There would be lots of adjustments, but she and Maxine were good at creating alternative ways of cooking foods.

Snake skin, and Joyce showing pineapple that grew in their yard.

Chapter 14

DEALING WITH LOSSES

Sad news! Life was difficult on a 'normal' basis, but then it could always get worse—for the missionaries as well as the Africans. For one thing, there was always the threat of war with neighboring countries. When Joyce and Maxine first went to Africa, they lived in the small country of Burundi for a year, learning the language. One of the ladies who shared a house with them was an African named Monika who worked at the Christian radio station. Now they received the devastating news that she and her whole family had been killed in the war that was going on there. People of certain tribes were targeted by other tribes. Joyce and Maxine could hardly believe what they were hearing. How could this be? Monika was such a good and sweet person. They figured that maybe because she worked at the radio station, that was perhaps the reason she was targeted.

There would be other situations of bad news. On one of their trips over to Katshungu station, they took a twelve-year-old girl with them who needed medical treatment, but she later died. Before she died, she gave a wonderful testimony of her faith in the Lord by singing songs she had learned in Sunday school. She told her family not to cry because she was going to be with the Lord.

One week later, they received more sad news while they were at Katshungu. One of the teenage boys back at Ikozi station had drowned when his canoe overturned in the river. His father was the dispensary nurse there at Ikozi. His mother was away on a trip, and they didn't know how long it would be before they could get word to her. The boy was the grandson of a big chief.

Another man at Ikozi had a large tree fall on him and had to be dug out from under it. It broke both of his legs, and the bone was sticking out of the flesh. That meant they had to get him to the doctor at Katshungu and then on to Lulingu. They had brought him in on just a stretcher (no ambulance), so they had to give him lots of pain medicine for the drive over that horrible 'road' to Katshungu— at night! Maxine set out driving the Scout with some Africans going along for help.

Seems like everything was happening at Ikozi, where they didn't have the medical help that they had at Katshungu. One evening, a woman was brought to them with her jaw out of place. Their dispensary nurse, who had just lost his son in the river, was not back at work yet. It was late afternoon and no one was on the radio, so they couldn't ask for advice. Sometimes a doctor or nurse could step them through a procedure. This time, they were on their own. Several people had gathered on their back porch, trying to pull her jaw back in place. They gave her some Anacin to ease the pain and told her she would have to wait until morning when they could get a nurse on the radio. Sure enough, the next morning, they got Evelyn on the radio from Katanti, and she gave Maxine play-by-play advice on what to do—more pain medicine first. Poor Maxine was just getting over a bad case of the flu herself, but she went to work on the woman's jaw. After three or four attempts, the jaw went back in place. Praise the Lord! The first thing the woman could say was, "I'm hungry."

With all the deaths and accidents happening, life could get pretty dismal at times. And to make matters worse, they were having trouble finding someone to work for them as a houseboy. Luxury, some may think? Not hardly. They couldn't get their teaching work done if they had to spend all day chopping wood for the wood-stove, hauling water and boiling it for safe drinking/cooking, baking bread, cooking meals, etc. Everything was done so primitively that it was very time consuming. And they needed someone dependable who they could trust.

I hated to have to write and give more bad news from home, but we had three different deaths in one month in our extended family—an uncle, an aunt, and a cousin. Even though the news was not always good, they begged for letters from home. And it was extra special getting mail because of how they had to get it—by mail drop from the plane. During one of those mail drops, they were visiting another village about twelve miles away, and they didn't want the pilot to miss seeing them. So they tied a sheet to a long pole beside their Scout and opened all the doors. The plane flew so low, it almost snagged the sheet. The wind in the sheet made it look like one of those windsocks at the airport. The Africans said that the 'flag' was pregnant. Time for a good laugh!

While they were at this particular village, they were encouraged by the meetings they were able to have with the people. They saw their need and hunger for the Word of God. One man came up to them and said, "We want you to come teach us more; we're still in darkness." After all the bad news that had been happening, this was encouraging to them. They were reminded that God does not guarantee an easy or safe life to those who serve Him, but in the end, "To God Be the Glory."

The rugged way of life was not easy on their bodies, and they needed to go to east Africa for better medical checkups. They drove over to Kampala, Uganda, to a Baptist Mission that had a good doctor.

Plane circling for mail drop.

Maxine had started having a very rapid heartbeat, so they kept her there for observation. When it came time to head back home, her pulse and blood pressure were still too high, so the doctor kept her there until they could find what was causing it and get it stabilized. That meant that Joyce would have to make the trip alone. She would have to get an African to go with her in case she had car trouble. She was glad to get back home, but she sure did miss Maxine.

One of the African women brought Joyce some cassava and some greens that they get from the forest. Joyce cooked them up and then invited the woman to eat with her. Since their fridge wasn't working, everything that was cooked had to be eaten. There was no way to keep leftovers. Joyce opened a can of sardines to go with the greens, and the two of them enjoyed a 'good' meal together. She also had baked some coffee rolls, so they had that for dessert. Joyce was tired after all her baking and cleaning, but she didn't get much sleep that night. The cat and a stink rat made a big ruckus up in the attic. The cat finally killed it but didn't eat it because it smelled so bad. Instead, it left it under Joyce's bed!!!

While Maxine was still gone, Joyce had to make another trip to some villages in an area where no missionary had been for twelve years. An African would always accompany her in case of car trouble, and he would take his bicycle in case he had to ride for help. Another would also go along to help with teaching the lessons. This trip would last for two and a half weeks, including sessions with the school teachers. The people were very receptive and thrilled that she came. They loaded her down with 'gifts' such as two goats, several chickens, dozens of eggs, peanuts, and plenty to eat while she was there. But one of the goats ate the lining out of the African's jacket, along with some soap. It also poked a hole through the plastic wash basin. They decided they would later kill the goat to celebrate whenever Maxine got back, hopefully in time for Thanksgiving. It was a young goat, so the meat would be tender. As it turned out, the goat got a reprieve until Maxine's birthday in February.

Another loss! They learned that the tractor had been lost in an accident. The driver had tried to turn around in a tight spot and went over a cliff. He managed to jump free and was not hurt after sliding twenty feet. The tractor slid fifty-five feet, and one wheel broke off and went down one hundred feet. Praise the Lord no one was hurt or killed. But what would they do now without that tractor? The men would have to go to the mining station to see if they could help pull the tractor out.

Even something as simple as picking lemons could be a major undertaking. They had sent an African out to pick some lemons from their tree. He came back saying there was a big, long snake in the tree! It crawled all the way to the top of the tree, and they worked for an hour trying to get it down. When they finally suc- ceeded, they speared it to kill it. It measured almost seven feet long! They were thankful that no one got bit.

One other close call with a snake was when Joyce was standing at the dining room table, mixing up something to bake, when she noticed that the cat on the couch was staring at the wall behind her. When she turned around to see what had the cat's attention, there was a big cobra crawling down the wall right behind her. She yelled for the African to come with his machete, but it had disappeared up into the ceiling. The Africans climbed up into the dark attic, found it, and killed it with their machetes.

Another medical emergency was when a woman was brought in on a stretcher and was very bad off. She had given birth to one twin, but the second one came a week later and died. She had lost lots of blood and was very sick. Joyce drove her over to Katshungu for further help. They were hoping that more of her family would come forward and donate blood; the husband's blood was the wrong type.

Devastating news!!! Pilot down! On March 20, 1973, their pilot, John, left Bukavu airport early in the morning headed east to Nairobi, Kenya. He was planning to sell the plane before heading to the States on furlough with his wife for their daughter's wedding. He was supposed to make radio contact at 7:00 a.m., but they never heard from him again. It was after midnight (1:00 a.m.) when a delegate from the American Consul came to deliver the news that John had crashed and was killed. Witnesses said it sounded like he had engine trouble. This news was so devastating to all the mission family, and even to me when I learned of it. He was the pilot who had flown me down into the bush on my first visit there. Now they all found themselves hurriedly making funeral arrangements. The pilot and his wife had lived and worked at the Uku station, and now plans were being made to bring the pastors from there up to Bukavu for the service. The people dearly loved John, and they wept like babies at his service. The missionaries quickly made a marker for the grave with the proper lettering on it. Joyce helped arrange flowers on a cross made from chicken wire, in addition to arranging three large pails of flowers. The service went very well, considering how quickly everything had to be arranged, and in Congo (at the time Zaire), that usually didn't happen. Now they had to go on with heavy hearts, trusting the Lord for comfort and guidance. A few years later, they would once again receive the sad news of a second pilot, Jack, who was killed when his plane went down, barely missing a group of people. Witnesses on the ground said he was desperately trying to steer the plane away from all those people.

After everyone else left Bukavu following John's funeral (first pilot killed), Joyce had to stay to see the doctor again. The pain was persistent in her side and severe at times. Now they were suspecting gallbladder problems. They gave her some medicine to take before the x-rays, and she had a severe reaction. They discovered that she was allergic to the iodine in the medicine. The x-rays showed that the gallbladder was okay, but the bile duct wasn't functioning properly, causing swelling and spasms and severe pain. This was also aggravating the colitis. The doctor gave her more medicine to help the liver produce more bile. Joyce joked that she had 'bad plumbing.'

Joyce eventually made her way to Nairobi, Kenya, where she was planning to meet me again. We had been making plans for months to meet, and this time, our dad was planning to go with me. But at the very last minute, we had to cancel our trip when the doctor said that Joyce needed to come to the States for more thorough checkups on her liver. We were all so disappointed but agreed it was the best thing to do. Joyce would not have felt like entertaining us over there. Our plans were put on hold for a while—several years, as it turned out.

Joyce flew to the States on the day that we had originally been scheduled to land in Nairobi. What a switch in plans! She was admitted in to Methodist Hospital in Houston, and they advised lots of rest. She stayed with me for a while and then later went to Kentucky to stay with our other sister, Carol Sue, who was living there at the time. It was out in the countryside and would be restful for Joyce.

After other doctors' visits and hospital stays, it was advised that Joyce should not go back to Africa yet. So the mission sent her out to New Mexico, where they had a station among the Navajo Indians. This was quite the opposite of Africa, including the people's personalities, but the extreme arid desert conditions worked out well for her allergies. She met new friends and even learned how to make Navajo fry bread. She spent several months there before heading back to their home office in St. Louis, MO.

Chapter 15

REUNION

When Joyce left Africa for this medical trip, Maxine had stayed behind to continue with the children's work and translation work. Now, two years later, it was time for Maxine's furlough, so she flew to St. Louis, where Joyce was staying. They were so glad to see each other again. They had a lot of catching up to do. The mission board decided that Joyce was well enough to return to Africa after furlough, so she and Maxine began their planning. They bought a little Ford Pinto to do their traveling for deputation. They had a lot of friends and church supporters who needed to be brought up to date.

After several months of traveling, they were thankful for no accidents or car trouble. The mission board gave the okay for them to return to Zaire (formerly Congo) once again. Joyce was overjoyed at the news and was reminded of the Bible verse, "Commit thy way unto the Lord; trust also in Him, and He shall bring it to pass" (Psalm 37:5). The next few weeks were spent packing barrels with all the items that had been donated to them while on deputation. Now was the time to stock up on things before heading to the bush again. And their car had to be sold before leaving the States. So much to do—no rest on furloughs.

After getting everything done, they flew from St. Louis to Washington, DC, to visit with Maxine's brother for a few days before leaving for Africa. They were so anxious to get back; Joyce had been gone for almost three years. But they were shocked when they reached their mission center in Bukavu to see how much of a jump in prices for food there was while they were gone. They joked that they probably should have brought more food than clothes with them. They also needed some furniture while staying at the mission center. The previous missionaries had moved out and sold most of their furniture.

But their stay in Bukavu would be short-lived. Instead of getting to fly down to their station in the bush, they had to once again go the opposite direction to the doctors in Nairobi, Kenya. Joyce was again having significant pains in her side, and Maxine was experiencing an outbreak of boils. Doctors were stumped as to what was causing Joyce so much pain. Finally, the tests revealed a duodenal ulcer. She would need LOTS of rest and to watch her diet. And the liver would continue to give problems, due to that overdose of malaria medicine that was given to her a few years earlier. Again, they were reminded of a Bible verse: "The spirit is willing, but the flesh is weak" (Mark 14:38).

While they were in Nairobi waiting for test results, Maxine's purse was snatched when they went shopping. The purse was later dropped but not until they took her wallet and money they had with them for grocery shopping. They decided to get out of the city and go out to another mission station about an hour's drive up into the mountains to stay with friends. There was a school for the missionaries' kids called Kijabe (pronounced key-JAH'-bee). One of the teachers there was one of Joyce's teachers when she had been at Bible college in Dallas, TX, years earlier. You never know when or where you will meet up with someone again.

All of the doctors kept insisting on mandatory rest for Joyce and for her to not go back to living in the bush. They strongly advised that she return to the States and get evaluated over there. So, on Sept. 17, 1977, she arrived back in Houston, TX, to stay with family. Doctors here did extensive tests and said that she had gone beyond the exhaustion point—she never fully recovered each time before going back. The doctor said that she would need twelve hours of rest each day for three months. That was not what she wanted to hear, but that's what her body needed. Her heart ached to return to Africa. Would she ever be able to go back?

After about seven months of rest in the US, doctors gave the okay for her to return to Africa. She would leave from New York in April of 1978, along with the widow of the pilot (John) who was killed a few years earlier. They arrived in Bukavu, Zaire (Congo), on April 18 and, two days later, flew down into the bush to Katshungu station. What a grand reunion!! Everyone was so excited to be reunited once again.

But—not everything was going smoothly. There had been serious church problems while Joyce was gone. Maxine had to fill her in on what all had been happening. The one dissident (the outgoing legal representative) who previously had caused a lot of strife was now spreading his lies and dissention among others—some even reverting back to witchcraft. This was causing a lot of tension on the station and making it hard for them to carry on their work; as if it already wasn't hard enough—roads closed due to bad conditions, no way to get gasoline, and food prices going up.

Fresh meat was not always available, and when they could buy some, it would be weighted down with any extra part of the carcass that could make the price higher. They would use salt to trade for eggs or whatever else they needed. One day, a little girl stood at their back door with a very broken egg in her hand that she wanted to trade for salt. But they decided that this egg was too 'incomplete' to be called an egg.

Now that Joyce was back, they were all anxious to get classes started again. By this time, Joyce and Maxine had moved into a larger house high up on a hill overlooking the station. She would continue teaching children's classes as well as teaching the women and girls sewing, usually on their large porch. She also needed to teach the men and women Christian Education so that they could relieve her of the workload. And she would also work at setting up a literature program to try to get supplies for them and teach someone to manage this program.

Maxine's main work was on the translation team, but she also worked in Christian Education. They would encourage their supporters in the States to send them their old Christmas cards that had pictures of the nativity scene or other Bible stories. These would be given as awards to the Africans for Bible memory. The Africans didn't have much, so they would treasure these pictures.

Joyce also planned a Sunday school picnic for the girls, probably the first of its kind in the rainforest. There were all sorts of relay races, including sack races, and instead of bobbing for apples, they bobbed for guavas. You use whatever you have. They had a light plant that ran on diesel fuel, so they had electricity for a couple hours at night. And they also were able to get some CB radios, which greatly helped with communication between the missionaries' houses. Now they didn't have to send notes back and forth with a runner. They were beginning to feel quite 'uptown' now.

Dad in Africa! Another reunion! Finally, in 1979, after having had to postpone our trip since 1973, our dad was able to make the trip with me. This would be my second trip, but his first. He immediately started looking around to see what he could fix. He was self-taught in carpentry, electrical work, plumbing, mechanics, and just about anything else, so he had plenty to do, including fixing their gutters that were practically falling off the house. The gutters were crucial for collecting rainwater. He could 'tinker' with anything and get it

Joyce's sewing class on front porch; pet monkey 'helping' Joyce type; Bible Institute building and Christian Education worker/teacher.

to work again, but it was very frustrating for him to not have a tool store nearby. He was tall, slender, and agile, and the Africans were amazed at how active he was. He even convinced them to let him go with them into the forest to cut a tree. I don't know who was more excited—Daddy or the Africans.

We, of course, took a footlocker loaded with supplies for Joyce and Maxine—many of the items were provided by the ladies at our home churches who gave a shower. We made it all the way down country without having to open the footlocker or our suitcases for inspection, which was rare. Our dad even took several harmonicas and had fun teaching the Africans how to play them, which didn't take much teaching because they were so musically gifted. He also took his saw and a violin bow to show them how to play that too. By bending the saw between his knees and sliding the violin bow along the edge of the saw, he could play any song. The Africans were amazed and said that he could 'make the saw talk.'

While we were there, Maxine had a bad fall. She had always joked that if she fell, there was a 'bounce on every ounce.' But one night while walking through the village, she tripped on a root growing across the path and fell head first. She fractured her jaw in three places and also dislocated it. They flew her out the next day to another station where she could get some relief, but it would be two weeks before she could get to Nairobi to have the jaw set and wired together! For weeks, every bit of food had to be pureed and drunk with a straw. Although very painful, Maxine always made the best of every situation. It was so hard at mealtimes to have to watch her drink her entire meal while we could chew ours. There are so many things that we take for granted, even chewing.

*House at Katshungu in need of repairs; Joyce and Maxine unloading footlocker
of supplies that Dad and I took to them; Dad working on repairing gutters; Dad
demonstrating how to play the saw.*

Chapter 16

MORE SETBACKS—YET MIRACLES

Once again, Joyce's abdominal problem would require taking furlough sooner than originally planned. Doctors in Kenya insisted that she needed more stomach surgery, and Maxine would also have her jaw checked. They arrived in the States on March 8, 1980, and immediately went to Mayo Clinic in Rochester, Minnesota. They were referred by friends to a lovely couple (Randy & Regina Harmison) who lived near the clinic and opened their home as a place to stay.

I flew up to be with them during Joyce's surgery. Of course, coming from Texas, I was not prepared for Minnesota winters. When I got off the plane in open-toe sandals and there was snow on the ground, they just about had a fit wondering how I would survive. I assured them that I would be staying inside. Even inside, I just about froze! Anything below seventy degrees is too cold for me. But the Harmisons were wonderful hosts who were very musical and kept us entertained. God graciously provided once again. We were very grateful for them.

After getting out of the hospital, Joyce and I flew home to Texas, where she could recuperate. Maxine flew to Kansas City, MO, to visit family and friends, as well as to Colorado and California. They would later be reunited to make plans to return to Africa. While they were here, they learned that the house in Ikozi where they first lived had been burned to the ground by the dissidents. Now they would have to raise funds to buy another kerosene refrigerator to replace the one lost in the fire, and also a wood stove. But they were thankful that they were not in the house at the time.

They had come home in March, and by December, they received word that they could start planning to return. They needed to renew their visas. This was always a process that meant waiting. They had flown to Maryland to visit Maxine's brother and to leave from there. On New Year's Eve (Dec. 31), they found themselves sitting for three hours in the office of the foreign embassy, waiting for a needed visa. Finally, the passports went by special messenger to the ambassador and then came back properly signed, just in the nick of time. Another miracle! You can't leave without your visas stamped in your passport.

They were relieved to see that all fourteen pieces of luggage got sent with them. There is always the possibility that some might get separated and get sent on another plane. Nine of the footlockers had been sent from St. Louis, where they had been stored for three weeks. They had been hurriedly packed and labeled (with a log rack for firewood brought at the last minute), and yet they all made the 10,000-mile trip to Africa practically unharmed. Another miracle!

After the long trip, going through several countries, they made their way back down to their station in the bush. Joyce had to be flown in, since she was still recuperating from surgery, but Maxine made the trip by car with others. Due to many landslides, it was a very arduous trek, but God made a way. It took a week to go the long way around (350 miles), and on the worst day, they only went nineteen miles. They got stuck ten times (thank goodness for the winch), broke two main springs, had multiple tire problems, and the starter went out on the Scout. That's why four-wheel drive vehicles are so necessary on those 'roads.'

How bad are we stuck this time?

Another grand welcome home! Many gifts were brought to show how glad they were to have Joyce and Maxine and others back— eggs, rice, peanut butter (homemade), baskets of firewood, etc. There seemed to be a sweeter spirit among the people this time. Joyce and Maxine were so glad to be back home. When out of Africa, they felt like a fish out of water.

Now that they were back, it was time to dig in again with all their teaching duties, translation work, and planning a Christmas cantata for the choir. That took a lot of time because Joyce had to translate the songs and make their extra syllables fit the music. They also planned a trip to Katanti (approx. forty-five miles away) for a seminar. They would ride on two mattresses in the back of the pickup truck because of the rough road. The only stop they made along the way was for the driver to hunt monkeys.

Maxine with some of the villagers; picture of message drum.

*To watch a video of the Africans singing, visit the
link below or scan this QR code.*

https://www.youtube.com/
watch?v=G72ti8XtkOI

By the latter part of the year, their kerosene refrigerator arrived that they had ordered. Even after many miles of overland transport, it arrived undamaged—not even a scratch! What a treat to have refrigeration again in the depths of the jungle. Praise the Lord!

Communicating by drum! The type of message drum used in their area by the Kilega people was a large, flat, hollowed-out wooden drum with a handle across the top that resembled a purse strap. It had 'low tones' and 'high tones,' depending on where you beat with the rubber-tipped mallet. The drum beat would be picked up about every five miles and relayed along the African 'telegraph' system. Early morning or late evening would be the best times.

The low and high tones would resemble the lows and highs in their daily existence. Because of Joyce's ongoing abdominal problem (liver damage caused by parasites as well as a duodenal ulcer), it was definitely a 'low tone' in her life. She would have to make frequent trips out by plane to Nairobi, Kenya, in east Africa. And moving from guest house to guest house while in Nairobi was also a 'low tone' for them. Maxine usually went too so that she could also get medical and dental needs taken care of.

The 'high tones' for them would be when they could return to their station in Zaire (which is now called Congo again). Even though the workload would be heavy and stressful, they were thrilled to be back. They had a pastor who came from another station to help Maxine and others with the translation workload. Even a wedding was planned and performed for an African couple, and they made a beautiful wedding dress for the bride.

To watch a video of an African wedding, visit the link below or scan this QR code.

https://www.youtube.com/
watch?v=0tHNBTIiPFw

Joyce and Maxine both had many verses underlined in their Bibles for assurance and encouragement during difficult times, especially when there was opposition against the church. One reference was Isaiah 42:6-7: "I the Lord have called thee in righteousness, and will hold thine hand, and will keep thee, and give thee for a covenant of the people, for a light of the Gentiles; to open the blind eyes, to bring out the prisoners from the prison, and them that sit in darkness out of the prison house."

And each time they had to leave for medical reasons or evacuation, they were comforted with such verses as Genesis 28:15: "And behold, I am with thee, and will keep thee in all places whither thou goest, and will bring thee again into this land; for I will not leave thee, until I have done that which I have spoken to thee of."

Was their work finished? Not yet. Even while Joyce was in Nairobi for medical reasons, she was able to continue in the work. For instance, she took advantage of being in the city to get copies made of literature that they needed for teaching, and copies of the translation work so that each person working on it had a copy. In spite of various hardships, they would continue holding teaching seminars. They figured that if the Africans were willing to walk many miles to come (some walked over one hundred miles one way), then the missionaries needed to 'feed' them spiritually with God's Word so that they could return to their villages prepared to teach their own people.

Besides teaching many classes, their days were filled with many other obligations—and many interruptions; there was always someone knocking at the door to borrow something or ask for advice. One of the mission's directors had come for a visit from the home office in St. Louis, and he said the missionaries needed to organize their time better. One missionary replied, "If you can organize our interruptions, we will organize our time."

At one time, there were only four ladies on their station; the men were either on other stations or on needed furloughs. So when a fierce tropical storm blew through and took the tin roof off two buildings, what could they do but wait for Jim to come from Katanti? And then he had to return and make repairs at his own station. The hard rainstorms were always taking a toll on their buildings. And it was so difficult getting more supplies, such as sheets of tin for roofing.

Our dad was able to make another trip with me over there in the summer of 1983, and he was more prepared this time and had a better idea of what he needed to take. He was able to help with making repairs on some of the buildings. We were there for their Bible Institute graduation ceremony, so I was able to help too with such things as posting grades on report cards. Graduation day was always a big event followed by a large outdoor feast under leaf-covered canopies over the tables. Much work was put into the event, including making choir robes for all those in the choir. Then the robes had to be ironed outside with a charcoal iron (no electricity) and then hung on long poles and carried down to the church, which was downhill from their house. Better not drop them! They took a lot of pride in making this a very special celebration. After all, in the middle of the jungle, this was very special.

Carrying choir capes down to the church.

After graduation, it was time for the graduates to head home to their respective villages, and for some, it was a long, dangerous trip. For four years, they had made their home there at Katshungu station, and now it was time to return to their families, equipped with biblical knowledge to teach and pastor their own churches. Later, two of the pastors had the opportunity to go with Joyce and Maxine by plane to a distant village. Now they could see the forest from the air, the same area they had trudged by foot that took twelve days! This was a dangerous trek because they would encounter everything from gorillas, elephants, cape buffalo, to other dangers. Now it was a breathtaking trip to be flying over that dense forest.

Slippery takeoff! With graduation over with for the year, it was time to get back to their regular schedules. They planned a trip to a distant village for a Christian Education seminar with children's teachers. Since that village was near a mining airstrip, the mission plane was able to fly them within a mile of the village. BUT—because of lots of rain, they had a very slippery takeoff. The pilot had to abort twice, and they skidded to the side of the airstrip. On the third try, they were able to get off the ground. The Bible verse on their calendar for that day was Exodus 3:12: "Certainly I will be with thee."

Another setback! All the missionaries had flown up to the mission center in Bukavu for a semi-annual field conference. While there, Joyce's health problem flared up again. From there, she flew on to Nairobi, Kenya, to have more tests done by her doctor there. After lab work and other tests, it was strongly advised that she not return to work in Zaire yet, but instead to work in an area where medical help was closer. This was devastating for Joyce because her heart was in Zaire with the Balega people. So after much prayer and checking into other options of where to work, it was decided that she stay in Nairobi and work on loan with CEF™ (Child Evangelism Fellowship) that she had worked with before. Once again, she had to return to her station to pack up her belongings and to delegate her workload to others. Hopefully, it wouldn't be for good.

But it eventually meant another trip to the States. Maxine was able to hurriedly pack and meet Joyce in Nairobi before leaving for another trip to Mayo Clinic in Minnesota. It was decided that they needed to return there to see what was going on since Joyce's last surgery. The results were much better than expected. It seemed that Joyce's body had a tendency to get adhesions after surgeries, and this was what was causing so much pain and discomfort. It definitely was a disruption (low tone) in her life. They both were able to have checkups and minor surgeries while in the States.

As in previous trips home, they would always combine medical leave with furlough and use the time to gather more support and supplies. This time, they would even take advantage of enrolling in one semester at Calvary Bible College in Kansas City, MO, while in that area. You can never have too much knowledge, especially when teaching. Joyce took some lessons to expand her training in piano, organ, and choral conducting. They joked that Joyce had to "face the music" every day. Maxine enrolled in English Composition and Cultural Anthropology.

Sad news from Africa! It's always hard to get bad news, but it seems even worse when you are so far away from 'home.' While they were here, they received devastating news from their station in the bush. One of their nurses, Betty Lindquist, had suddenly died! She had been in Africa for many years, originally serving with her husband and then continuing on to raise her three children there after his death. He had been one of the original missionaries to settle in that area. What a blow to all there! Everyone loved Betty. She always had a good sense of humor in spite of all the hardships. Her death left only three missionaries there—her son, Jim, and his wife, Louise, and another nurse, Lydia F.

Joyce and Maxine were really feeling the tug to return to their station. They could hardly wait until time to go back and help. They preferred driving through all the mud in the jungle compared to driving on frantic freeways here. But they were able to accumulate quite a few large items during this furlough to take back with them—a radio transmitter, a new 1100-W generator, an electric typewriter, an electric sewing machine, etc. They were deeply grateful to all who helped to supply these items and to those who gave financially to cover shipping expenses and other needs such as a place to stay while traveling here in the States.

Another reason they were anxious to get back to Africa was the fact of not being used to all the snow while they were in the Kansas City area attending college. What a drastic shock for two 'Africans.' They were having a severe winter that year with fresh snow falling every week for five weeks in a row. They each had taken a 'good' fall, but no broken bones. Maxine said that their college classes were only a "hop, slip, and a bump" away.

Time to leave again! Friends and fellow students from the college came to help pack boxes, weigh baggage, send some items parcel post, rent a U-Haul truck, load it, and then unload it at the airport. All hands were greatly appreciated! There were forty pieces of baggage, and it ALL arrived in Africa with them—nothing got lost. However, Joyce's portable organ was badly damaged, but she was hoping a fellow missionary could fix it. She would really need it for her work with the choir.

As many times as they crossed the ocean, no two trips were alike. This flight would only take them to Burundi, the small country next to Zaire, and the rest of the way (five to six hours) would be by truck—big enough for forty pieces of baggage. A truck and driver were located to drive them from Burundi to the Zaire border.

Fiasco at the border! Border crossings in Africa can be quite eventful. This time, they wouldn't let the driver cross, saying he didn't have proper papers. Then the driver said that the arrangement had been to only take them halfway. So Maxine caught a ride with another driver to get to Bukavu on the Zaire side of the border for help. Joyce stayed with the baggage to wait, but when help didn't come before the border closed at 6:00 p.m., she decided to have a driver take her and baggage back to where they had stayed the night before. She got back at 9:30 p.m. in spite of having to talk her way through four barriers and two half-drunk truck drivers.

Meanwhile, Maxine was on her way back with two vehicles and a missionary, Mark, to rescue Joyce and baggage. But no Joyce, and borders were closed. They had to spend the night in their vehicles swatting mosquitoes. When Joyce never showed up, they became concerned and went back to Bukavu to notify authorities.

Joyce had now located another truck and driver and headed for the border again. Along the way, they met another big truck with a load of tourists, and they had been told to be on the lookout for Joyce. They even had a letter from authorities in Bukavu to the American Embassy in Burundi to look for Joyce. When she saw the letter, she felt like a fugitive. She didn't realize everyone was looking for her. After changing trucks and drivers a few times, she finally made it to Bukavu well after dark. What a reunion they all had!

After a week at the mission center in Bukavu, they were able to fly down to their station, Katshungu, and had another big reunion. They were so glad to be home again and immediately began setting up their household again—awaiting the arrival of the rest of their boxes.

Chapter 17

MAJOR PROJECTS AND UNDERTAKINGS

Palm tree plantation! Don't be misled by the word 'plantation' and think of a large house in the southern United States or elsewhere! This plantation would be a grove of trees planted on the hillside. Since the Bible School students who would be enrolled in the college would be living there for three or four years, they would need all the help they could get for sustenance. So Joyce had an idea.

The type of palm tree that grew in their area had large clusters of nuts that grew in the top of the tree. A skilled African would climb a pole ladder, carrying a machete, and would carefully chop out the big cluster (called a palm head) and let it fall to the ground. One narrowly missed Joyce's head once when it fell by itself without being cut. After the hard work of chopping into the head and separating the nuts, they would be boiled in a large container. A reddish-colored oil would be produced, and this oil was used for cooking. Chicken cooked in palm oil was a real treat. They could also sell this oil and have some income for the students.

So Joyce and Maxine began planning. They would supervise the Africans in clearing off the backside of the hill that they lived on. Then they ordered some small trees that could be brought in and planted. Lining up the rows was as simple as stringing rows of string. They started with seventy-five trees and eventually grew to more than two hundred. Then stick fences had to be built around each young tree so that the goats wouldn't 'groom' them. It would take four to five years for a tree to produce.

Sheep project! In the jungle? Maintaining the control of forest growth was more and more difficult, so Joyce had another idea. Why not bring in sheep to control the growth? This would also provide meat from time to time for the Bible Institute families. After doing some research, they found that Dorper sheep would do well in their area; they are a South African breed. Due to limited grazing area, it was best to have no more than about ten sheep. More fencing would need to be built, and the woodshed behind their house would need to be cleaned out so they could be brought in at night. A shepherd would be paid to keep an eye on them during the day while grazing. Part of their salary would be paid from the sale of the palm oil. The Africans were wary of the large rams that never missed a chance to butt them, so they made a wooden gate to corral them in a corner in order to retrieve their food pans.

Fishpond project! At the bottom of their hill there was a fishpond that had become pretty much overgrown with forest growth. Joyce had another idea of how to make this a source of food and income. The pond would have to be drained in order to clean it out. This project was turned over to the Bible Institute students, since it was for their benefit. Even the women would help to clean it out. Then it was restocked with tilapia fish. This not only helped their diet, but also added to their meager source of income. Eventually other fishponds were developed.

Hydro-electric plant coming? Not only had they received word that four more families were coming to the field to help with the workload, but they also got word that another couple would be returning from furlough with a hydro-electric plant. This would be

Palm tree plantation and fish pond.

Clearing the hill to plant more palm trees.

Harvesting the palm heads and drying the nuts.

Building fence for sheep and goats;
Joyce with her 'babies' including twin kids.

a major project to be installed at the waterfall near their station that would provide electricity for the first time to the hospital and also the Bible Institute village, and eventually the missionaries' houses. Jim Lindquist would be overseeing this project, with occasional ones coming from the States to help. But it was often frustrating to the helpers to not have the materials they needed. First, the dam had to be built, but the torrential rains gave problems, causing the water to go over the dam before planned. Jim had researched how to build a hydro-electric plant, and gradually various parts were imported from the States and assembled on-site. Over time, a handful of men working together were able to construct the generator and turbine machinery, test it, and get it all running. Electric poles were a challenge to move around and install without cranes. A small pickup truck would drag each long pole to the desired location, and then groups of men devised a series of ropes and man-power to hoist the poles upright into large, manually-dug holes. This project required a lot of hard work, but it was worth it to finally have electricity in the jungle.

To watch a video of the hydro-electric plant,
visit the link below or scan this QR code.

https://www.youtube.com/
watch?v=ySeTGhvriJU

These were all major projects in addition to the daily ongoing ones, such as teaching in the Bible Institute, Sunday school classes, sewing classes, translation work, printing out lessons, etc., which took lots of time. And all of these activities would get interrupted on flight day. The households were thrown into chaos on those days as everyone scrambled to prepare outgoing loads and mail, as well as checking the incoming loads. They needed to get the truck quickly

Hydro-electric plant built at waterfall; raising poles for wiring.

loaded and be at the airstrip three and a half miles away before the plane landed because the pilot usually had a short turn-around time before taking off again. If time permitted, they packed a quick sandwich or something to give to the pilot. Flight day also meant that someone at both ends of the trip had to 'flight follow' on the radio until he landed. Weather could change quickly and drastically alter his schedule.

Maxine on radio for 'flight following.'

Unloading the plane was also time-sensitive—go over the list and see if everything came that was ordered over the radio and then quickly reload. Everyone had to be backed away a safe distance as the plane took off, although the kids enjoyed feeling the strong wind from the revving engine blowing on them. The trip from the airstrip into the village was awful, especially after a hard rain that washed over the trail. One time, the water was up to the bottom of the truck's doors. The driver had to maneuver as best as they could while trying to protect the load—not easy if you had a load of eggs that came in on the plane.

Unusual flight! Due to a previous injury, Joyce once again had a painful flare-up in her left leg. While trying to make arrangements to get the mission plane in, God intervened with a helicopter! It was not 'scheduled' to land there but was nearby on another mission when the weather suddenly changed and he needed a place to land. When an opening appeared in the clouds, the pilot quickly landed on their soccer field, which originally had been designated for a helicopter field but was never used for that—yet. After the pilot got his bearings and found out where he was, he said he would be back in fifteen minutes to get Joyce. That was probably the fastest that she ever packed. But the helicopter ride was quite an experience, and all who watched thought so too, especially the kids who were jumping with excitement.

The trip to Nairobi meant that more tests and scans were necessary to pinpoint the problem. The results indicated immediate hospitalization and surgery. Scar tissue had formed and caused swelling around a disc, trapping nerves. While on the plane flying to Nairobi, there was a Gideon Bible that had been placed there, and it opened up to a verse in Mark (6:31), which said, "Come ye yourselves apart into a desert place and rest a while." How fitting to see that verse at that particular time. Sometimes God has to remove us from our work to rest and to "restore our soul" (Psalm 23:3).

After surgery, she was fitted with a back brace to wear whenever she was up and around. She would need to wear it for several months. How would she be able to continue her work? She was determined though, and was assisted by Maxine being her 'candy-striper' nurse taking care of her.

I was able to make another trip over there, this time accompanied by our cousin Sherwood. He was a carpenter, so he had lots of projects to tackle, one was to build a new front door for their house. It seemed like there was no end to replacing or rebuilding something. On our last night there, a fierce cyclone blew through. We thought the roof was coming off! With no electricity, we couldn't see what was happening but could only hear the tin on the roof being banged up and down and the windows breaking. We all got separated in different rooms and didn't know if everyone was okay.

Finally, when it calmed down, we were able to light kerosene lamps and check out the situation. The walls had shaken so hard that some of the bricks around the fireplace in the kitchen had fallen. Since it was our last day there, we had to scramble to clean up everything, finish packing our suitcases, and get out to the airstrip before the plane came—if it could land. A chainsaw had to be used all along the way to remove large trees that had blown over across the roadway. We could see the path that the storm had cut through the forest. We were so thankful that everyone was safe.

Our trips to Africa always culminated with a trip to east Africa to take in a game park—there are several not far from Nairobi, so each time, we went to a different one. You hire a tour guide who drives for hours out across the plains to a lodge. This was always relaxing and quite the treat. You never knew what you would get to see because some animals are more prevalent in certain areas than others. Our favorite was the lion, and we saw plenty of those. We had a rare opportunity to see two Cape Buffalo fighting. Even the African driver said he had never witnessed that. He stopped the Land Rover, and we sat very still and quiet so as not to attract them to us. They are very dangerous animals and can overturn a vehicle, so we were glad to ease our way around them.

Project Jeep! Joyce and Maxine had been saving up to buy another vehicle, and they were finally able to buy a used four-wheel-drive Suzuki jeep in good condition. It was smaller than their previous vehicle but was easy to handle. But it was almost short-lived when Maxine had a close call. While driving to a weekend church conference, a rickety old bridge collapsed under the vehicle, leaving it 'gripping' the bank with only its front wheels. Praise the Lord for

Sherwood building new door; clearing the path after storm.

the winch on the front end that pulled them up onto solid ground in a matter of minutes before almost losing the jeep. Joyce was not allowed to drive for a year after her back surgery, so her rides in the jeep were limited, usually only around the station.

Christmas music preparations! Due to being so isolated in the forest, preparations had to be planned way in advance. The Christmas cantata especially took a lot of preparation but was thoroughly enjoyed. Besides translating the words and music, Joyce also had to deal with the problem of 'the beat.' There was the tendency for the old ways of witchcraft and the use of rhythm sticks. But after one of their seminars, over one hundred gave up their sticks and declared "no more of that." For the Africans, Christmas was very special and was not taken lightly—all emphasis was on Christ, not gift-giving. The church would be packed with 700 people. The missionaries would celebrate later with an English service and sharing a meal together.

Fiftieth Anniversary! The year 1988 marked fifty years since their mission began working in Congo, so plans were started early for that celebration. Home Office personnel would be coming from St. Louis, so preparations would be extensive. It would be combined with the Bible Institute graduation; therefore, a large feast would also be prepared. The history of the mission would be acted out in skits held outside on the soccer field to accommodate all the people. It was a huge celebration. The theme was "To God Be the Glory." Combined with it would be the celebration of Maxine's fifty years of service in Congo (also called Zaire). The mission had plaques made commemorating both occasions.

Translation work! This was a very tedious and painstaking job of translating the Bible into their local dialect. One by one, another section would be completed. It was very important to have some of the Africans helping and giving their input. Their dedication and sacrifices were greatly appreciated, especially since many faced

*Maxine giving keys to Joyce to drive again after surgery; Joyce leading choir for
the mission's fiftieth anniversary celebration.*

much opposition. The pressures of culture can be very strong. One dear African, Eric, came on his bicycle from Katanti, forty-five miles away, to help with the work. He wore out his shoes, so Joyce and Maxine bought another pair for him. When they presented him with the new pair, he cried. All he could say was, "For me? For me?" The following year, they learned that Eric had suddenly passed away. Everyone was devastated at the news! He was deeply committed to his work of helping with translation, as were others who also took the work very seriously. They would meet with the missionaries and go over it word for word, hour after hour, day after day. Years later, when it was finally printed in their own language, there were tears of joy!

To watch a video of harvesting rice, etc.,
visit the link below or scan this QR code.

https://www.youtube.com/
watch?v=SOp3hchDjZA

To watch a video of life in the forest,
visit the link below or scan this QR code.

https://www.youtube.com/
watch?v=2Zz-gVApPds

Chapter 18

TRAVEL WOES AND SORE NOSE

Travel was always an issue to be dealt with, whether in Africa or on furlough in the States. There would be tons of preparation before setting out; therefore, you were already tired before you even started traveling. And due to the slow pace of processing passports and visas, this had to be carefully planned and coordinated with flight schedules to make sure you had your passport in hand when that time arrived. Passports had to be sent all the way to the capital in Kinshasa for processing, and that was about 2,000 miles away. Many times, the passport would be received the day before departure. Too close for comfort!!

Being down in the bush, travel was definitely an issue because of weather. They had to allow extra time in case of fog or rain. You didn't want to miss getting out in time to catch an international flight out of the country because flights didn't leave daily, and it was a nightmare to reschedule. It could make a difference of a day or more, and that would mean having to find temporary housing along the way.

On one trip out from their station heading to Nairobi, Kenya, for dental work, they had quite an eventful trip. First, they had a rather marginal take-off over the treetops, and then they ran into very bad weather. After flying seventy-five minutes (instead of forty-five), they landed on a half-overgrown mission airstrip way out in the 'middle of nowhere.' When the storm let up, they retrieved their baggage from the small mission plane, only to discover that some of it had gotten wet as a result of leaks in the cargo area. And the lid had come off the peanut butter jar in their lunch bag. The toothpaste had also flipped its lid, and the tube of hand cream had expanded beyond restraint. Their supply of stamps got wet, making the glue most effective, but not necessarily where they were intended to stick.

They had to overnight there until the storm passed, and that meant carrying their wet baggage on their heads from the plane in to the mission station. The next day, they flew out through many clouds to their mission center in Bukavu before going on to Nairobi. After that rough flight, even the bumpy roads of Bukavu felt good. Another Bible verse came to mind—Nahum 1:3 says, "...the Lord hath His way in the whirlwind and in the storm, and the clouds are the dust of His feet." Along the way, they picked up a patient with appendicitis who needed urgent care. You never knew who you might share a flight with.

Even in the States, travel was tiring, and there would be a readjustment into civilization. They would need to carefully plan their route so as to visit as many of their supporters as possible along the way. Even with plans, things don't always go as planned. On one trip, after driving all the way to California, they arrived to find that their meeting had been canceled and no one told them! Seemed that some people didn't realize what driving across the desert in extreme heat meant. And there was usually an abundance of car trouble, having purchased a used car to drive while on furlough. But on one trip, after traveling over 6,000 miles and encountering fog, snow, rain, and a severe dust storm, they escaped car trouble that time without even a flat tire. One couple in Oregon even furnished snow chains for their car.

They would make the most of any situation, and while driving through one town in California, Maxine spotted an ice cream store— her weakness. They quickly turned around and found a parking place. After coming out with their ice cream cones, Joyce noticed a policeman walking up behind Maxine. Since Maxine didn't see him, Joyce began telling her in Swahili to warn her. The policeman told them that he had witnessed them making an illegal U-turn. They were horrified! But after hearing their story of just coming from Africa, he kindly didn't give them a ticket. That was almost one expensive ice cream cone.

There were good times and not-so-good times, but God always provided someone along the way to help them and to provide an oasis of rest for them. One particular time was when a dear couple offered their ranch as a place for them to 'hide out' for a while and recuperate. It was outside of Scottsbluff, Nebraska, and was a perfect place of quietness for them. There was a separate mobile home on the property that was not being used, so the owners offered it to Joyce and Maxine to stay as long as needed. And shortly after arriving there, three packages arrived for them—a computer, a printer, and a bundle of books. What a special gift from friends in California. The computer was very compact, only weighing fourteen pounds and very easy to pack for travel.

While in Nebraska, Joyce would need more surgery for stomach problems. The stomach was not emptying the food, but then the surgery caused a large hematoma mass, causing a blockage problem, which meant being readmitted to the hospital. Poor Joyce always said that her abdomen looked like a road map due to all her surgical scars. Being out at the ranch in Nebraska was a good place for recovery.

While on another trip through Indiana, they planned to visit Joyce's college-days friend, Loopie. By the time they reached Loopie's house, the side of Joyce's face and her nose were swollen. They didn't know what was wrong, but Joyce said it itched really bad. She told Loopie to get a flashlight and look up in her nose and see what it looked like. Loopie said it looked all infected and had lots of tiny water blisters. By the time Joyce could get to a doctor, they put her in the hospital right away on an IV for a couple days due to a serious fungus. We teased her about having 'jungle rot.'

Joyce's body was wracked with physical ailments, from stomach surgeries to back surgeries. Every surgery would only create more scar tissue that would require more surgery. It seemed like a vicious cycle, but because of the severe pain, it could not be ignored. She had to be carried to the airstrip in Africa one time on a mattress due to the pain. Even an air flight could be excruciating, so when she had to fly to Wheaton, Illinois, one time because of a herniated disc, she had to lay on a thick sheepskin for padding. God provided three seats abreast on the commercial plane so she could lay down, and the airline was very accommodating.

Joyce was always reluctant to have to leave, and one time, the mission pilot joked that the plane had a hard time getting off the ground because Joyce was dragging her feet. Again, she was reminded of a verse in Psalm 57:1: "Be merciful unto me, O God, be merciful unto me; for my soul trusteth in thee; yea, in the shadow of thy wings will I make my refuge, until these calamities be overpast."

Another surgery in 1994 took her to London, England, where she was referred to King's College Hospital for surgery to remove adhesions caused from previous surgeries. Once again, the Lord provided friends there to stay with while recuperating—someone we knew from our hometown in Hitchcock since she was eleven years old. She (Shirley) was now grown and married and living in Oxford, England, with her husband and three children. Her husband, David Shotton, was a professor at Oxford University, and they graciously opened their home for Joyce to stay with them until she could return to Africa. Joyce and Shirley enjoyed catching up on old times. I was also able to stay with them overnight while on layover on one of my trips to visit Joyce in Africa. It was so good to see Shirley again.

One flight out to Nairobi was especially 'interesting.' Stormy weather caused the radio transmitter to go out. The alternator went out with a quick flash and a bit of smoke coming from the dash of the plane. Because of no radio, they had to fly past the tower and 'wave' the wings several times to signal landing. It sure felt good when they were finally on the ground again safe and sound. Jeremiah 32:27 says, "Behold, I am the Lord, the God of all flesh; is there any thing too hard for me?"

Returning to Africa after furlough was always quite an ordeal because of all their baggage. Commercial flights would get them as far as Kigali, Rwanda, and from there it was a five-hour trip by truck through the mountains to the Congo border. It was a beautiful drive through tea plantations, but the road was not too good. With all their baggage, they had to hire two extra vehicles sometimes.

As the caravan of vehicles started out over the lush green mountain-side, one of the small vans kept overheating, so they had to keep stopping for water. Then first and second gear didn't want to coop-erate, and on one long, steep hill, the van just couldn't make the grade in third gear. Joyce had another idea! Why not turn around and try to back up the hill? As the driver backed up, Joyce leaned out the other window and directed traffic. People weren't sure if the van was coming or going. After reaching the top of the hill, they turned it around and continued on their way. A trip that should've taken five hours took eight hours instead.

Travel to other villages was always eventful. Often it required crossing a crocodile-infested river while sitting in a dugout canoe. You sat so low in the canoe that it looked like the water would come over the side any minute. The current was so strong that they would have to 'pole' along with the current. Joyce was able to film some of it, which was quite breathtaking!

One of their Bible Institute students had a close call on the river while going to a Christmas conference. He and twenty-one others climbed into the large dugout canoe with all their baggage, including a bicycle! Their student had a large zipper carry-on bag, weighing twenty pounds, with five Bibles and several New Testaments to sell at the conference. The river was way over its banks, due to consistent heavy rains. The paddler would first go upstream a bit, staying close to the banks, then cross over and let the current take them downstream to the other side.

However, this time, the river was so swift that it swept the canoe into the cable, which is usually high above the ferry. The force of the water against the cable tended to tip the canoe, so the men managed to lift the heavy cable over their heads to the other side of the canoe. Then they were swept into the ferry, and the canoe began to sink. Before it went under, they were all able to get onto the ferry. While standing there, being thankful to be alive, they saw the zipper bag with all the Bibles pop up. Another canoe came to collect the owner of the bag, and then the chase was on to catch up with the bag that was being swiftly carried downstream. They succeeded in grabbing it, but because of so much weight, it had to be pulled to shore, where they could grab a branch and pull the bag into the canoe without tipping over. All the Bibles had taken on very little water and were able to be sold at the conference. What a testimony to all who saw and heard of how God saved His Word from the depths of a raging river and made the Bibles float!

Even when they traveled by truck or jeep, it was not easy. One time, they were going to a village, and the weeds and brush had grown over the 'road.' Having no air conditioning in the truck, they had to leave the windows open, and the weeds were beating in and thrashing them. Joyce again was able to get some good video of it

Dug-out canoes and log bridges.

but later discovered how scratched up the jeep was. Due to her back situation, she had to sit on lots of padding when making these trips. They would get out and walk when they came to a boggy spot and let the African driver drive through.

Just going the three and a half miles from their station to the airstrip could be quite the experience—you never knew what might happen along the way, so they took with them whatever tools they thought they might need. While Maxine was making a trip out in the little Suzuki jeep (with no brakes or reverse gear), she came to a washed-out spot that required building some kind of a bridge to get across. She had to wait for the men to bring boards. Good thing she had brought along some strong forest vine to tie the logs together, since there was no hardware store nearby.

The Africans were accustomed to walking long distances, since that was usually their only mode of transportation. They were impressed when Joyce and Maxine or any other missionary offered to walk a few miles to another village to hold a seminar. In return, Joyce was amazed when one of their former Bible Institute students returned on foot from his village ninety miles away, along with his fourteen-year-old son, to pray for Joyce after one of her surgeries. This was a tremendous encouragement for Joyce and also a display of deep concern that the Africans had for them. Events such as this made all their efforts worth it.

To watch a video of a dug-out canoe ride,
visit the link below or scan this QR code.

https://www.youtube.com/
watch?v=xictHd579vo

To watch a video of the roads through the forest,
visit the link below or scan this QR code.

https://www.youtube.com/
watch?v=XV4uYYGVTQA

Chapter 19

HUMOR AND
RELAXATION AMID WOES

As mentioned before, whenever we would go over for a visit, we would be treated to a time of relaxation out at a game reserve in Kenya. In 1990, while Joyce and Maxine had to go to Nairobi for medical attention, they asked me if I could manage a quick trip to visit while they were there. It was easier to get to Kenya than it was to go all the way down into their bush station, so I was able to make quick arrangements.

This time, I had someone else to go with me—our youngest sister, Sue. We had a lot of laughs as we watched her trying to adjust to African culture. Even though camping is not her preference, she was willing to make a stab at it. This time, the game reserve that we visited had large tents on cement slabs with a porch on the front for relaxing. We would go to the lodge for our meals and enjoy quite a spread of food including many kinds of tropical juices. We tried to convince her that this place was one of the nicer ones, but she was counting the days when she could be back in her own bed.

At night, guards would roam the area to make sure the wild animals didn't come too close. The zebra and some of the other animals would come to graze under the lights for protection from the lions. One night, we heard the snorting of a lion not too far from our tent. We were glad for the fence around the tents and for the guards. Most of the time though, the only sounds were those of the various kinds of birds. It was peaceful being so far out.

On another trip, I took one of our nephews, Jon, with me. Unlike my younger sister, he was quite the opposite and was a daredevil to try anything. We left home right after his high school graduation in 1993. He was able to go all the way down to their station in the bush with me. He was 'all eyes' with excitement as we flew over the jungle in the small plane. He towered over the Africans, since he was around six feet tall, and they were amazed at his height. He was a basketball player at school, so he quickly bonded with them, even though they played mostly soccer.

To watch a video of the flight down-country,
visit the link below or scan this QR code.

https://www.youtube.com/
watch?v=oY9wbic-jzs

Even with the language barrier, they would manage to communicate most of the time. And they would convince him to try some of their 'delicacies,' such as grub worms cooked in a tin can over the open fire as they sat around it. He had many stories to tell when he got home, such as how they made shoes from old discarded tires. Before he left, they talked him out of his socks and baseball cap, even though the socks needed washing. They were thrilled to get anything, and they loved to barter. The hot tropical days were eased with cooling off at the swimming hole in the river just up the road. We would pack a lunch and have a picnic. There were large vines hanging from the tall trees, so Jon could 'swing like Tarzan' and drop into the water. The water was ice cold coming down out of the mountain.

And of course, the trip ended with a visit to a game reserve in Kenya. Joyce, Maxine, and I shared a tent, and Jon had his own. They were nestled under some trees a short distance from the lodge. They were on cement slabs with zip-up doors and windows. There were lots of monkeys overhead in the trees, and the guards warn you not to feed them because they become a nuisance. Sure enough, one day, we were calling to Jon to go for lunch at the lodge, but he couldn't get out of his tent. He had given a cracker to one lonely little monkey, and before he knew it, the monkey 'put out the word' and the whole community was down from the trees and hanging on Jon's tent so that he couldn't get out. All he could do was peek out the window. One monkey was even reaching under the tent flap to try to get another cracker. He knew where those crackers were coming from! We all had a good laugh before calling the guard to chase them off and rescue Jon.

There were other times when a good laugh would ease the rigors of life in the bush. One Sunday morning while I was there, we were preparing to leave the house to walk down the hill to church service. Many people had already gathered there to sing, and their singing rang out over the quiet forest. Just as we were about to walk out of the house, someone brought an injured baby bird for them to care for. Since time was limited, they quickly grabbed a mesh colander and turned it upside down and put it over the bird on top of the cabinet so the cats wouldn't get it until we got back from church. That particular Sunday, some of the other missionaries were coming for lunch. When we walked into the kitchen after church, the bird was still there. Jim spotted it and asked, "Joyce, is this your idea of pheasant under glass?" We all doubled over with laughter!

The Africans would also add times of laughter just by their expressions of situations. One day during one of their tropical downpours, Joyce commented to their worker that with all that rain, they would be growing web feet like a duck. He laughed, and then she asked him what they called a duck's web feet. He said, "Oars," and then it was Joyce's turn to laugh.

Another comical expression was from a child during a children's meeting. One of the teachers asked the question "Where is God?" and the child said, "In Heaven." Then the teacher asked "Where is Jesus?" and again the child said, "In Heaven." When the teacher asked, "Where is Satan?" the child said, "In the forest." They had a good laugh out of that one.

Traveling from country to country was also interesting. Each time you changed planes, you had to fill out cards of disembarkation to show with your passport. One of the questions asked was "What denomination are you?" and they would just put "Protestant." While in a bank in Nairobi one day cashing travelers' checks, the teller asked Joyce how she wanted the money. But when the teller said, "What denomination?" Joyce quickly said, "Protestant," without thinking. When she saw the look on the teller's face, she realized what she had done and quickly explained. Maxine and I had been waiting in the lobby, so when Joyce came and explained everything to us, we laughed so hard that the armed guard looked at us suspiciously, wondering what we were up to. We quickly left.

Communicating with one another could often be misinterpreted, even for the missionaries who knew the language. On one of my visits down into the bush, Joyce decided to take me walking around to take photos. As we walked a little way down the pathway toward what they called the crossroad to a little outdoor market, we were met by a soldier who spotted my camera and stopped us to ask Joyce something. I didn't know what he was saying, and Joyce wasn't quite sure either. He pointed to my camera and held his other hand sideways against his throat, just below his chin. I saw Joyce's facial expression change, and I wondered if he meant he was going to cut our heads off if I didn't give him my camera! It felt like my heart stopped for a few seconds! All he was trying to say was that he wanted me to take a picture of just his head so he could get a passport. Phew!!! Felt like I lost a few years of my life on that incident!

There could even be a moment or two of laughter during wartime. On one of their evacuations to Nairobi to wait out the turmoil, I was again able to visit them while they were there. They had become pretty 'shell-shocked' from sudden noises. One day, we were sitting out in the yard on a bench of the apartments where they were staying when suddenly there was a loud bang. They automatically dove under the bench, only to later discover it was just a backfire on a large truck passing by. They looked around to see if anyone saw them, and then we had a good laugh.

Chapter 20

SAD NEWS FROM HOME

It is never easy to receive bad news, but when you are 10,000 miles from home and receive urgent news, things have to kick into high gear to make all the necessary arrangements. Our dad had been diagnosed with terminal cancer after surgery for a small tumor in the bladder. It had spread to the pancreas and other surrounding organs. The prognosis was not good, and the chemo treatments were making him so sick, so he decided not to continue with them. He didn't want his last days to be spent being so sick.

Joyce was able to arrive home only one month before his death. She was able to stay with him at home and help our stepmother, Mary, to care for him, along with Hospice care that would come to administer medications to keep him comfortable. It was so hard to watch him wither away to skin and bones. It is a helpless feeling.

Daddy passed away on Sept. 24, 1992—just six days after his seventy-ninth birthday. The funeral service was very special, with poems and tributes to a long-time railroad man. Someone gave us the words and music to the hymn "Life's Railway to Heaven," so we included that on the program.

After just two months at home, it was time for Joyce to head back to Africa. This was not a planned furlough, so it had to be cut short. She was to connect in Paris with another missionary who was also heading back after furlough. They would be able to make the rest of the trip together.

Joyce made it back in time to work on the Christmas music program. She was pleased and thankful to see how one of the African men had handled things while she was away. And she had another surprise—one of her sheep presented her with a new baby lamb. This would now make a total of eight in their little flock.

The following months would bring more sad news from home, as Maxine learned of the death of one of her brothers. It was sudden, and Maxine was not able to make it home. And then Joyce learned of the deaths of a couple (Mr. & Mrs. Roush) from our home church. They were like family to us. She had died suddenly of a heart attack, and two months later, her husband died. We were all in shock! We had known them for many years in our church, and our youngest brother had married their daughter, so they were part of our family. And Mrs. Roush had also been a very close companion and friend after our mom died.

The next couple of years would bring news of other deaths—relatives, friends, and supporters. The end of 1995 brought news to Joyce of the death of our stepmother, Mary. Just three years earlier, Joyce had stayed with her during our dad's illness and death. Mary was a good gardener, and Joyce had enjoyed time with her while picking vegetables from her garden. Being of Czech descent, she was an excellent cook and gave Joyce a lot of tips on how to grow and cook vegetables.

Whether on furlough or on the field, there would be other deaths, either from accidents or illnesses. The son of one of their Bible Institute teachers was killed when a tree fell on him. He had gone to help his grandparents cut an area for their rice garden. A felled tree started slipping down the hillside toward him (they can bounce), and it hit him on top of his head and shoulder, killing him instantly. They had gone about sixteen miles into the forest, so it was late when they arrived back at the station, carrying the body in the moonlight.

This was the third young man to die in a month's time—the other two were from chronic illnesses. There was another incident that could have been fatal when a rabid dog wandered into their yard but got away before anyone could kill it. Good thing their own dog had been vaccinated. But there was an outbreak of ten cases of people being bitten. They always had to keep the rabies vaccine on hand.

Cancer is a terrible disease that shows no partiality. One year, they lost one of their older Bible Institute students after a brief bout with cancer. He was a third-year student, and his two sons were first-year students. The dad had insisted on enrolling first to get a head start on his sons. However, the Lord chose to promote him to Glory before finishing.

There would even be deaths among their animals. The driver ants could move in at night unexpectedly and strip the chickens to the bone. Even though the chicken coops were up off the ground (chickens like to roost), they had to pour diesel fuel around the legs of the coop to keep the ants away. They would even pour it around the doors of their houses to keep them out.

Even the sheep were at risk. Usually, if there was a commotion at night in the sheep pen, you knew something was wrong, and you'd better go check. If it wasn't ants, it might be a snake. Two of their rams had to be butchered because of snake bite. Even while the sheep were out grazing, there was always the risk of snakes. One day, the shepherds killed a large viper that had fangs about two inches long! Then two days later, some squawking chickens alerted them to a six-foot cobra. Life in the forest had to be of constant vigilance.

Large viper that was killed.

To watch a video of snakes,
visit the link below or scan this QR code.

https://www.youtube.com/
watch?v=Z8NircsHqps

Chapter 21

WARS AND OTHER INTERRUPTIONS

Besides not being easy, life in the bush could be very unpredictable. But they diligently continued on with the work that they felt called to do. The small Bible Institute was seeing growth each year. Some were coming from many miles away to study and then return to their villages, equipped with knowledge of the Scriptures to teach their own people. While they lived there, the men and their wives participated in the church choir. One year for Easter, they had thirty-three voices. As Joyce led the choir, she could see the expressions on their faces change as they sang "Christ Returneth," eagerly anticipating the day when they would be redeemed from such a hard life.

Things did not always go smoothly. The dissident group that had separated from the church was growing and causing many problems, disruptions, and lots of strife. The situation began to get serious as the group planned to take over the station. Some lives were even threatened. A poison arrow was found near the house where a guest had stayed. One day, the group of 300-400 people came in like a flood—with weapons, planning to take control of everything. But the missionaries and locals closed up everything and stayed locked in their houses until they passed on. They were reminded of several verses of assurance in the Bible. Jeremiah 1:19 says, "And they shall fight against thee; but they shall not prevail against thee; for I am with thee, saith the Lord, to deliver thee." Also, Psalm 46:10 says, "Be still and know that I am God; I will be exalted among the heathen, I will be exalted in the earth."

In the middle of all these disruptions, they also experienced a strong earthquake in Oct. 1993 that caused quite a lot of damage to their houses. They had experienced tremors in the past, but this was a strong quake. Trees in the forest shook and some fell. Some men who happened to be in canoes on the river at the time said the quake created waves that pushed them to the shore.

The biggest quake hit on October 4, with an aftershock on October 8. Plaster came raining down on Joyce's bed, and she didn't know which way to run. The outer wall had a huge crack, as did other walls as well. Their office room had separations in the walls, and the floor cracked so bad that now it was split-level. The brick chimneys suffered great damage also. It would take major repairs to make their houses safe to live in, but they were thankful that no one was hurt. This greatly increased the need for making more bricks. The hydro-electric plant down at the waterfall was knocked out of commission and would be out for five months—meaning no electricity.

In addition to earthquakes, they would often have cyclone-like storms pass through. One hit one night while they were visiting their Katanti station about forty-five miles from their home. It pretty much took the roof off of the little brick church.

Joyce wrote that the heavy blowing rain, fierce lightning, and hail made an eventful evening. Because of all the rain, it brought the river up to flood stage with very swift waters. They would need to cross it in a canoe. They had borrowed life jackets but weren't real sure how to secure them. They could only hope that if they were put to the test, their head would stay above water and not their feet! They thanked God for His watch care once again.

Katanti church damage from storm.

Earthquakes weren't the only 'rumblings.' There were also tales of government unrest and economic problems, either in Zaire (later renamed Congo again) or neighboring Rwanda. While Joyce and Maxine were in Nairobi for medical checkups, tensions on the border between Zaire and Rwanda finally erupted into gunfire between ethnic groups in the border city of Bukavu, where they needed to go. Flights down country would be temporarily canceled as the mission plane would be grounded—being based in Nairobi, the plane couldn't cross borders into other countries. This made travel very difficult, and Joyce and Maxine were told to stay in Nairobi, Kenya, until things settled down.

After a while, they were given the all-clear to return to Zaire. So they proceeded to charter a planeload of supplies to fly them back to their station in the bush. But they didn't quite make it—they were stopped in Bunia (up in the northeast) and had to stay at another mission's guest house for about three weeks. All women and children were brought together here for safety. While there, shooting erupted, so everyone stayed in with the curtains drawn, sitting on the floor to avoid being hit by stray bullets. It was decided to move everyone to a safer place.

The next morning, a caravan of five Land Rovers with thirty people, baggage, and food supplies left in a convoy with two armed military soldiers for protection. They headed out of town and went high up into the hills to another station (Bogoro). The road was so terrible with holes that a couple times, they thought the vehicles would over-turn. But once they got there, the view was beautiful overlooking Lake Albert. They stayed there for two and a half weeks. At least they were able to have radio contact with those who got trapped in Bukavu and down country at their station. Jim Lindquist had opted to stay with their people in the bush to help care for things there and give moral support. His brother, Tom, and his wife, Kathy, and their oldest son were trapped in Bukavu. They had planned to leave, but when fighting started, they were not able to get out. Also in Bukavu were Richard and Kathy McDonald, who ran the Christian radio station and stayed to protect it. They too were trapped and spent days crawling around on the floor to stay out of sight and dodge flying bullets. All of their lives were in danger, especially the McDonalds, as the soldiers set up their arsenal in their backyard.

After a couple weeks, it was decided that all should leave the country. Before leaving the country, those who had fled to Bogoro had to leave and stop once again at Bunia, where they had just left, due to fighting. They would need to get their passports stamped, showing they had officially left the country. As they flew over the velvety green hills, their hearts ached at the thought of leaving the country where they had served so long. Now they could only wonder what would happen to those left behind.

Once they landed in Bunia, there were several hours of 'negotia-tions' in trying to clear the mission plane that had been grounded. While waiting for their baggage and computer to be checked, one of the military men asked Maxine to show some papers for the computer. She thought they meant to produce something in print of the work being done on it. So she produced some copies of the translation work on the Kilega New Testament that had been done so far.

When the man saw it, he asked what language it was. Maxine answered, "Kilega," thinking no one up in that area knew what it was. But the man called another soldier to come over and asked if he could read it. The soldier's eyes lit up as he saw part of the Bible in his own language! With pleading eyes, he asked if he could keep the printout. Maxine was able to give him six of the books from the New Testament—much to his delight. What a thrill to know that God says in Isaiah 55:11, "So shall my word be that goeth forth out of my mouth; it shall not return unto me void, but it shall accomplish that which I please, and it shall prosper in the thing whereto I sent it." Even wars cannot stop God's Word from spreading. They were so thankful that they had been able to bring their laptop computer with them because of all the translation work that had been entered into it.

Eventually they were all flown to Nairobi, Kenya, in east Africa, hoping to be safe. The flight was very rough, going in and around several storms. Joyce stated that it seemed as if the sky was 'weeping' with the sadness in their hearts. They finally landed in Nairobi just in time before the 6:30 p.m. deadline for small planes. But before the mission plane could even land, they had to wait for a large military plane to be moved. It had landed at the private airport, where it shouldn't have been.

They felt like gypsies—always on the move. Although they were now safe, they worried about Jim, who chose to stay with their people down in the bush and also the others who were not able to get out. Reports were coming out of lootings and killings. Many were fleeing to the forest to hide. One African family got separated while fleeing and for three weeks didn't know where their children were. They were later reunited and relieved to know they had been saved by an aunt who took them with her. Another African man was reunited with his children after learning they had walked approximately 250 miles to get to Nairobi.

Due to the thousands of refugees fleeing from Rwanda and Zaire, it was difficult navigating and finding housing to rent. But they soon found an apartment building there in Nairobi where they could all be together, as different ones (including Jim) made it out of Zaire by the end of April 1997. He had not seen his family for months, or even been able to talk to them. Rich and Kathy McDonald would be the only ones remaining there to protect the radio station. Missionaries from other areas were also being evacuated, so housing was scarce. They would remain here for several months, each one comparing harrowing stories of what they had been through. I was able to make another trip over to visit with them while they were 'holed up' there, and to celebrate Christmas and Maxine's fiftieth anniversary of being in Africa, even though it was in 'exile.'

They all ached to be back at their station with their people. They always felt bad about having to leave, but the nationals couldn't leave. One beneficial thing about being in Nairobi at this time though was that they were close to the office of Wycliffe Bible Translators, and they were able to get much valuable information and help toward getting their Kilega translation printed.

The word was finally received in July 1997 that it was settling down enough in Zaire that Jim felt he needed to try to get back. So they loaded up a truck, and he and his family headed back. Others headed for the States for furlough, so that left Joyce and Maxine in Nairobi by themselves. Joyce had been battling a bad case of typhus, so she couldn't leave yet. But by August of 1997, she and Maxine were finally able to make it back to Zaire, but only to their mission center in Bukavu on the border. It felt so good to be closer to home, where they could at least have radio contact with their people down

Maxine's plaque awarded for her fifty years of service in Africa.

in the bush. Even the airport workers gave them hearty welcomes to show how glad they were to have them back. But they were saddened to hear of how many were gone—either killed or had to flee. They were thrilled to see Rich and Kathy McDonald, who had stayed through it all. They were so thin, but safe, and they seemed so hungry for fellowship with other missionaries. They had a lot of 'catching up' to do.

By September of '97, they were able to finally get back 'home' in the bush. Oh, what rejoicing to see everyone again. They had been gone for a year, due to all the problems. There were many, many stories that they all had to tell. Now there was a mammoth job of cleanup and work schedules. The workers needed to be paid for the past year, but with a shortage of money, they had to just use the barter system most of the time. There was a steady stream of visitors coming to greet them and to especially be a part of Maxine's delayed fiftieth anniversary celebration.

The hydro-electric plant was damaged, and floods from heavy rains caused landslides that had taken out some poles, so the only electricity was from their generator (as long as gasoline lasted) or from solar panels, if there was enough sunshine. Jim had a massive job ahead, since he was in charge of all maintenance. Due to the elements of the rainforest, there was always plenty that needed repairing.

And there were constant repairs needed on their vehicles. One day, as Joyce headed down their hill in the Suzuki jeep, she smelled gasoline real strongly. When she stopped at the bottom of the hill, she noticed smoke coming from the hood. She quickly jumped out and tried to keep others away in case of an explosion. They yelled for help, and soon the guys were running with containers of water to throw on it. Everything under the hood was well charred and melted. There was even a burned trail down the hill behind the jeep. Apparently, there had been a slow leak. They were so thankful that no one was hurt.

As if that wasn't enough excitement for one day, that night, they had another battle with driver ants in the yard. And to add to that, there was a snake about five feet from where Joyce was sleeping! But the cat discovered it and alerted them. Never a dull moment!

That was nothing compared to what was about to happen. Little did they know what was coming from the neighboring country of Rwanda—the 'Big War'! Everything would drastically change.

Chapter 22

THE BIG WAR–TRAPPED IN THE FOREST

The problems caused by the dissident group that was trying to take over the property would be overshadowed by what was about to happen. Problems in the neighboring country of Rwanda to the east had erupted into a full-scale war. Many thousands would be killed, and many others would flee into Congo to try to escape and hide. There was no warning; they just heard the news one day (Aug. 2, 1998) that all airstrips were closed. That meant that the mission plane could not come from its base in Nairobi, Kenya, to bring them supplies or to rescue them.

Joyce and Maxine were trapped in the forest! All other missionaries were either on furlough or had gone out for medical reasons. Any other time, they felt safe down in the bush with the Africans because they were 180 miles from the border and the 'road' was practically impassable due to landslides. They felt that the rebels would never be able to penetrate the forest to reach them. This would prove to <u>not</u> be a deterrent this time! Since the city of Bukavu was right on the border, it got hit first. There was much looting and destruction. Rich and Kathy McDonald would remain in Bukavu to try to protect the radio station. They had a satellite phone, as did Joyce and Maxine, so they could stay in touch with each other.

It was only a few days later when hundreds of Congolese government troops began making their way through their station as they fled the oncoming army from Rwanda. On Aug. 11, about seven soldiers came up to their house with guns, rockets, etc. and said they needed to 'borrow' the mission truck. It would never be seen again. Shortly after that, they also took the radio transmitter, and things continued to deteriorate. But Joyce and Maxine had been able to have the Africans hide their satellite phone by burying it. They didn't want to lose that because that would be their only contact with the outside world.

Often many shots would be heard, and Joyce and Maxine would hit the floor to dodge bullets. On the morning of Aug. 16, about six armed soldiers came into their house around 9:00 p.m. unannounced and demanded money. Maxine tried to alert others on the CB radio, but one of the soldiers grabbed her arm to stop her. She jerked her arm loose. Although this was a very scary moment, they did not harm her. But they insisted that she get the money or they would kill her! They followed her into the bedroom to see where the money was hidden. They left after grabbing about $400. Because the government soldiers were very underpaid or not paid at all, they thought it was okay to rob or steal.

The next day, a soldier came to their back door, preparing to throw a grenade in if he didn't get some food quickly. Fortunately, their Bible Institute director was able to calm him down, and they were able to get some food for him. But in another incident, one young man was shot in the leg three times because he couldn't produce a chicken quick enough. Another two men were executed as spies right near their station when they were caught with hand-drawn maps of the forest for the rebels.

Soldiers were stationed for about four weeks on their station. Joyce and Maxine stayed mostly in or near their house during that time. Due to armed soldiers coming to the house interrogating them about using radio transmitters, they felt that they could not use any communicating device. So the last time they had contact with anyone was on Aug. 30, 1998, for six weeks.

Again, they were comforted by Scripture; Joyce underlined in her Bible the verses in the Old Testament book of 2 Chronicles 20:15,17: "Thus saith the Lord unto you, Be not afraid nor dismayed by reason of this great multitude; for the battle is not yours, but God's." And verse 17 of that same chapter says, "Ye shall not need to fight in this battle; set yourselves, stand ye still, and see the salvation of the Lord with you."

On Sept. 7, the soldiers decided that they were all leaving—with much fanfare of gunshots. But two soldiers lingered behind at their house for four hours. They came with loud voices, telling Joyce and Maxine to come out. But they were hesitant to come out of their house because the soldiers were in position in their front yard to fire with machine guns! One of their workers (who had been staying in the house with them) went to open the door, and the soldiers quickly forced their way in to check things out, probably hoping to find more money. They had brought two dead ducks to be cleaned and cooked, so two of the workers had the 'privilege' of doing the job. Joyce said ducks had never been plucked so fast!

That night, their workers who were still on the station were afraid for any of them to stay in the house. So they decided to take Joyce and Maxine into the forest for the night to hide. At about 8:30 p.m., they all slipped out of the house and down the back hill through the palm tree plantation in the moonlight. After clearing the second fence, they went a short distance into the forest. Their guards got them settled down for the night under some tarpaulins. It was a beautiful moonlit night under the lacy canopy of trees. The only real disturbance was mosquitoes and heat; although they did have a brief scare when they heard noises. It turned out to be just someone moving too much under the tarpaulins they were hiding under. This incident would be a preview of what was to come soon.

The next day, they cautiously made their way back to their house. They heard that about thirty government soldiers had returned to protect the area. But around noon that day, they heard the first big boom not too far away. The rebels were advancing! The first rocket was soon followed by more rockets and heavy shooting as they advanced. Joyce and Maxine quickly drew the curtains, locked the doors, and headed for the pantry to hide under mattresses that were stored there. Joyce commented to Maxine that they "might not get out of this one." But the Lord gave them a calm spirit as they prepared to possibly meet Him that day! However, He chose to bring them through this one.

The shooting was terrible, and noise from the rockets at close range was deafening. One soldier was stabbed and shot as he tried to flee. When the shooting calmed down, they heard a knock on their back door. Was it friend or foe? It was one of their Christian Education workers coming to check on them. They quickly brought him into the house, and he stayed with them through the night. The next morning, another worker showed up at the back door, and oh, how glad they were to see who had survived. They showed Joyce and Maxine a spot in the high grass behind their house that was all mashed down where they had been hiding to keep watch on them to see that they were safe. Such loyalty!

Three days later, on Sept. 11, a large plane was flying over, seemingly harmless, when all of a sudden, a second plane came over the mountain range. It roared right over their house and shortly thereafter dropped four bombs just beyond the station. They didn't have time to run but instead just braced themselves against the shaking kitchen wall, as the house shook violently. Two of their workers made an Olympic dash toward the palm tree plantation, clearing two fences with incredible speed!

When the dust cleared, some of their station leaders came rushing up to their house and said, "It's time—Let's go!" Their Bible Institute director, Masudy, had told them that they could go to his hideout in the forest when the time was right. Now was the time! Several of their workers helped them quickly pack up what they would need, and then they escorted Joyce and Maxine into the forest, carrying bundles on their heads. They hiked about one and a half miles deep into the forest, crossing streams by walking on a fallen tree, and by climbing up and down mountainous terrain. When they got to the 'camp,' there were already others there who had set up their living quarters. It looked like a refugee camp—and I guess that's what it was. This would be their 'home' for several weeks.

After a few days, Masudy had several of the men build a separate shelter for Joyce and Maxine by using tarpaulins stretched over poles. They also used mats, plastic bags, and whatever else they had to keep the rain off of them. They even had a solar shower rigged up in the trees to provide warm water for showering. They would end up staying here for a month, so they needed to figure out ways to 'rough it.' They even brought with them a wire shelf from their refrigerator to use as their outdoor stove to cook on. But there was always the constant fear of the wrong people seeing their smoke, so the fires would need to be kept small.

Joyce would need to hike back to their house for more supplies, so she would always take an African with her. They would not let her go alone. They would make sure the coast was clear. It would take at least forty-five minutes to an hour, one way, to hike up and down hills, through mud, and across streams. Maxine would stay at the camp, as this was too rough for her (she was seventy-five at the time). Thanks to a flight just a month before, they had food staples back at their house, including plenty of rice from the previous harvest. There were also local greens from the forest to cook, and the boys enjoyed fishing in the ponds. Once in a while, there was fresh meat or chicken; otherwise they had some canned meat. Preparing foods and boiling drinking water was quite a chore because their workers all had their own responsibilities, but they managed. Everything had to be cooked on an outside campfire.

After a month of sneaking back and forth to their house, the food supplies were running low. They had pretty much emptied everything out of their kerosene refrigerator back at the house. The only thing left was a jar of pickles, so they had pickle juice sandwiches. Their cook had been able to make bread on one of their trips to the house.

Kangela baking bread.

After having no military in the area for a month, they gradually moved from the camp back into their house. But they had heard from one of the Africans that there was a savage group of cannibals that were coming to butcher and eat the missionaries! They realized

To watch a video of their refugee camp,
visit the link below or scan this QR code.

https://www.youtube.com/
watch?v=t1JRlE0SOKo

that they desperately needed to get out, but how? The soldiers had taken their truck. Any other means of getting help was miles away—too far to walk.

Joyce remembered the buried satellite phone, so she had one of the Africans go dig it up. She mustered up enough courage to quickly try to reach the outside world before anyone caught them with a phone. The phone wouldn't work! Joyce wondered if someone else had tried to use it and messed it up. Each time she tried to access it with a code or password, nothing would work.

Meanwhile, back in the States, we and the mission headquarters in St. Louis were in touch with the US State Department, trying to find a way to rescue them, or even find out if they were still alive. The news reports coming out of Congo were not good, and we had not heard from them in six weeks. The mission told the State Department about the satellite phone they had and to be on the alert for any activity on it. So when Joyce was trying to access it, they were noticing the activity on it and decided to track it down. An operator finally came on the line and asked Joyce for her name. She said, "I can't say," fearing that the nearby rebels would pick up on the radio frequency. The operator then asked, "Where are you?" and again Joyce said, "I can't say." Joyce was finally able to convince the operator who she was, and the operator stepped her through getting access to the phone.

It was a warm, late-summer day in Texas when I just 'happened' to stop while mowing my yard and came in for a quick drink of water. The phone rang as I was entering my house, and when I answered it, I was shocked to hear Joyce's voice! After six weeks of nothing! I yelled her name, and she quickly told me not to speak too loudly, as there were 'others' not too far away who could pick up any radio activity. I asked where they were, and she could only say, "At the house," without giving away their location. At least I now knew where they were and that they were alive. She said they desperately needed to get out, but without a vehicle, they guessed they would just have to start walking. When she indicated which direction they would go, I told her they couldn't go that way because that was where the news was saying the rebels were coming from. All of a sudden, Joyce said she had to go, and she quickly hung up! I was left hanging without any more information and not knowing when or if I would get another call from her.

I immediately called their mission headquarters in St. Louis to notify them. When Jill, the secretary, answered the phone, all I could say was, "Jill, they're alive!" She quickly bounded up the stairs and burst into the room where they were having a meeting and blurted out the news. Soon the phone lines were jumping with activity, as we all had so many to notify, including the State Department. Another urgent contact would be the mission in east Africa that provided plane service for missionaries in remote areas. Joyce and Maxine knew them personally, having used their services many times, so they had their phone number. But with all the borders closed, how could they get in? Little did Joyce and Maxine know how fast plans would be made to rescue them, above and beyond what they could ever imagine. The urgency was increased when Joyce said that she had discovered a painful lump in her breast! People all around the world were praying, and we were receiving hundreds of calls and e-mails from people who heard of their predicament. God would answer in a miraculous way!

In a couple of days, I received another phone call from Joyce, and she was able to fill me in on some more details of what they had been through while hiding in the forest. She told of the damage to their station when the bombs were dropped; one bomb landed in their fish pond and made a huge hole where all the mud was piled up on one side. When describing the bombs on the phone, she would just have to say, "Large eggs." Thankfully, no one was killed from the bombs.

Joyce was also able to make phone contact with the mission in Nairobi, Kenya, that had the plane service to let them know of the situation. From then on, things began to rapidly fall into place to arrange for their rescue. They received word by phone that their day of rescue would be Oct. 24 at 1:00 p.m., and they would need to be out at their airstrip—three and a half miles out. Not knowing who, what, how, or any other details, they would need to scramble to pack up what they could and start hiking out to the airstrip, trying not to alarm too many people, lest their plans be thwarted. They were sick to think of having to leave their people, not knowing if they would ever see them again. They chose a select few to tell and to have them help carry their things out to the airstrip.

The last phone contact with the mission in Nairobi was at 11:00 a.m., confirming that the plane would be landing at 1:00 p.m., so they had to hurry and walk the three and a half miles to meet it. But with the borders still closed, how could a plane from Kenya get into Congo? When they got to the airstrip, there sat a small plane—with an African pilot! Who was this, and where did he come from? No time for questions; they just knew they had to hurry and load the plane and go. But after loading the plane, the engine wouldn't start!

Finally, the pilot got it started, and they took off. They soon learned the pilot's name was Ted and the plane was his own private plane—within the borders. It was a small Hawk-XP, and the XP stood for extra power, but Joyce said it stood for extra prayer because that's what it took to get out of there. They weren't airborne long before they encountered a terrible rainstorm with lightning, hail, and heavy rain beating in through the vents. The pilot told them that they were right over the area where the rebels were hiding with weapons that could shoot down an aircraft, so he quickly took the plane to higher elevation. Praise the Lord even for a rainstorm that engulfed them and drowned out the sound of their plane. Once again, they were reminded of the verses in Psalm 27:1-4 that say,

> The Lord is my light and my salvation; whom shall I fear? The Lord is the strength of my life; of whom shall I be afraid? When the wicked, even mine enemies and my foes, came upon me to eat my flesh, they stumbled and fell. Though a host should encamp against me, my heart shall not fear; though war should rise against me, in this will I be confident. One thing have I desired of the Lord, that will I seek after; that I may dwell in the house of the Lord all the days of my life, to behold the beauty of the Lord, and to enquire in his temple.

After about twenty minutes, they were out of the rainstorm and eventually landed in Goma up on the northeast side of Congo. But how would they get out of the country, with all borders closed? An African doctor (who had previously treated Joyce) met them at the airport and whisked them across the border, telling the guards that it was a "medical emergency." Once across the border, they saw the mission plane from Nairobi waiting with two pilots to take them to safety. They later learned that the African pilot who came to get them out of the bush had never flown to that area before and didn't know where it was, but after being told that there were two women who needed to be rescued, he said he would take the risk! How could all these factors have been arranged other than—God! "But this happened that we might not rely on ourselves, but on God" (2 Corinthians 1:9).

It was so good to see those pilots from Nairobi and to be reunited with friends when they landed there. The wife of one of the pilots even had sent a lunch for them of fruit, carrot sticks, and cans of soda, knowing they had had a long day. They were so grateful to have some decent food. They were able to get refreshed and rested while spending a few days at the home of one of the pilots and his wife. Then they hastily made flight arrangements to get to the US as soon as possible. They arrived in Houston, TX, on Oct. 31, 1998, and were met by most of Joyce's family. Oh, what a reunion! To God be the Glory! After having to hide in the forest for a month, they looked pretty haggard and thin, and their hair was yellowish from being in the smoke of the campfires for so long, but we were so thankful they were now home.

Although they were now safe at home, the battle was not over. Joyce would need to see a doctor as soon as possible regarding the large lump in her breast. We were able to get an appointment right away with an oncologist. Sure enough, the news wasn't what we wanted to hear—it was a malignant tumor. They started her immediately on chemo treatments to shrink the tumor before they could do surgery. She was already in frail condition, and the chemo treatments took a toll, including losing all her hair. But she quickly adjusted to a wig.

After several weeks of chemo treatments, surgery was scheduled for a mastectomy. The surgery was successful, and the doctor felt pretty confident that all of the cancer had been removed, but radiation treatments would follow just to make sure. The treatments also kill the appetite, and that was not what Joyce needed. So it was a long process of getting her back on her feet. But Maxine, her co-worker, had fared pretty well through everything (considering she was seventy-five years old at the time), and she was determined to be Joyce's nurse. As everyone who has been through the cancer 'ordeal' knows, it is very hard on family and friends. But we were receiving encouragement from many people around the world who were praying.

By the fall of 1999, Joyce's follow-up checkups were going well with good results. They wanted to be able to return to Congo to finish packing up their things that they had hurriedly left down on their station in the bush. They would not be able to stay down there, but they hoped to live at their mission center in Bukavu, which is on the border and would be safer in case of evacuations.

The doctor finally gave Joyce the okay to return, so they hurriedly started gathering supplies and making flight arrangements. They wanted to be back in time to celebrate Christmas with all their friends in Congo. We had to keep reminding Joyce to slow down when she would complain that her side was hurting. We thought it was too soon after surgery to be packing barrels. We didn't know at the time that it was an underlying symptom of something else.

Chapter 23

THE FINAL TRIP HOME

On Dec. 1, 1999, we were once again saying our goodbyes as they boarded a plane in Houston to take them back to where they called "home." It was a difficult farewell, knowing what they had been rescued from and not knowing what they were returning to. Along the way, they met up with two other missionaries, Jim and Louise Lindquist, who were also returning. They all made it to Bukavu, along with all of their baggage, including the much-protected translation work. The Africans were overjoyed to learn that they had come back, after all that they had been through. Even the border guards were glad to see them. There were many tearful reunions as they all shared their horrifying stories of what had happened. It was so good to see Rich and Kathy McDonald again, who had endured through everything to keep the radio station on the air.

Then began the job of cleaning up the area where they would be staying. The house in Bukavu had sustained quite a bit of damage from all the fighting and looting. Good thing they took extra supplies back with them because everything that had been left there was now gone.

Christmas came, and they were so glad to be back with their friends there, if for no other reason than to give them moral support.

Joyce's last Christmas in Africa (with Kathy McDonald & Maxine).

But Joyce developed severe pain in her side shortly after Christmas and had to be flown to Nairobi for medical attention. The x-rays and scans revealed something in the liver. She didn't suspect anything, since those liver spots had been there for quite some time from previous medicine. But the doctor kept insisting that she needed to get to the US for better treatment. She was dismissed from the hospital but stayed in Nairobi for a couple of weeks to recuperate.

When she had to be readmitted to the hospital, things began to really get dire, as doctors kept insisting that there was a large tumor in the liver. They were having to drain fluid from her body every couple of days. This would make it very difficult to schedule a flight home because it would take two days including layovers. But arrangements were made, including having an African nurse accompany her and Maxine on the trip. The nurse was willing to come because she had family living near Houston that she could visit. Praise the Lord for His arrangements!

We were told not to meet them at the airport; instead, an ambulance would be transporting her to the hospital near us, and we could meet them there. When the ambulance arrived and wheeled her in, we were shocked to see her condition! Her abdomen was greatly extended, and her skin and eyes were very yellow—indicating liver problems. They immediately paged her oncologist, who had treated her for the breast cancer. He couldn't believe she was back because he had just given the okay for her to return to Africa.

He quickly came and reviewed all the reports that she had brought from the Nairobi doctor. He was shocked to see the size of the tumor—the cancer had returned with a vengeance! He called us into a side room from where Joyce was and gave us the dire news. Because it was the liver and so advanced, there was nothing that could be done. We were so blindsided with shock, we couldn't say anything when he asked if we had any questions.

We slowly went back into her room, where she had already been told the situation. She seemed less concerned than we were—evidently already knowing, because Maxine later told us that Joyce wanted to stay in Africa to die there. When she arrived home, she was very much awake and coherent, but that quickly changed in a few days when she suddenly slipped into a coma one night while we had gone home to get some rest. A couple of days later, on Feb. 17, 2000, she was gone—to her final resting place. No more frail body, no more traveling back and forth across the ocean, no more problems. We were devastated and in shock that it happened so fast! Joyce had always pulled through so many other times. This would leave such a void in our lives now, especially for Maxine.

We came home to start making funeral arrangements and to start notifying everyone, including those in Africa who thought she was just coming home for a doctor's visit. What a shock for them too! We were told later that they had three days of mourning and services for her. Even the border guards remembered her. The pastor here from a local church quoted these verses at her service: "I have fought a good fight, I have finished my course, I have kept the faith; Henceforth, there is laid up for me a crown of righteousness, which the Lord, the righteous judge, shall give to me at that day..." (2 Timothy 4:7-8a). As Jesus said in one of His parables, "Well done, thou good and faithful servant" (Matthew 25:21).

Maxine stayed in Texas with me until I could make arrangements to escort her back to Africa. I would go to retrieve the remainder of Joyce's things, but Maxine would stay to continue helping with the final stages of the translation work that she had spent so many years on. Later, she would come home on furlough for a short time and then make one more trip back to Africa accompanied by co-missionaries Jim and Louise Lindquist.

By this time, age and the hard life in Africa was taking its toll on Maxine, and the mission insisted on her retirement. She, like Joyce, wanted to die and be buried in Africa, but the mission said that wasn't possible. She eventually settled into a Christian retirement home in the Kansas City area where she was from. I would fly back and forth from Texas now and then to help take care of her needs and to visit.

As time went on, dementia set in, and we realized that she could not stay in her small apartment any longer, so she was moved downstairs to their medical facility. I received a call one day saying that I should come as soon as possible—she was slipping into a coma. That was the fastest I have ever packed and arranged a flight from Texas to Kansas! I barely made it—she passed away that night. I hurriedly had to make funeral plans and try to notify as many of her supporters as I could. Pastor Henry Winkelman offered to come all the way from Burney, CA, to participate. His church had taken part in supporting Maxine the entire time she had been a missionary.

It was freezing cold with a strong wind blowing across the Kansas prairie as we made our way out to the small cemetery where Maxine would be buried next to her parents. She had already purchased a plot and made arrangements for a headstone. At the funeral service, we sang one of Maxine's favorite hymns, "I Love to Tell the Story." She truly did love to tell the story to the Africans, both young and old. She and Joyce had both taught many classes and especially loved telling the children. Over the years, many had come to hear about the Lord from their teachings from the Bible. They had answered 'the call' and endured the hardships. The Lord never promised that it would be easy, but they remained faithful. Acts 20:24 (NIV) says, "However, I consider my life worth nothing to me, if only I may finish the race and complete the task the Lord Jesus has given me—the task of testifying to the gospel of God's grace." Philippians 1:21 says, "For to me to live is Christ, and to die is gain." And Psalm 116:15 reminds us, "Precious in the sight of the Lord is the death of his saints."

A few years earlier, I had received a letter from one of their pastors telling what Joyce and Maxine meant to him. He wrote, "*I am a student of Joyce's. I became a believer in 1952, before Joyce came here. When I heard about this work of Mama* (title of respect), *I hunted for her and I heard her explanation; light now came to be able to go ahead with the work of God.*" He thanked the churches and people here in the States for sending them to minister to the people in Africa. He added, "*Because of this, we are happy with the work of Mama Joyce and Mama Maxine. Continue to pray for them and don't become weary of their needs. Regarding Joyce, my family accepts her. God knows how to choose a brave person—even when she is sick, this Mama is patient. Even in war times, this Mama holds on to her call from God.*"

"Well done, thou good and faithful servants!"

179

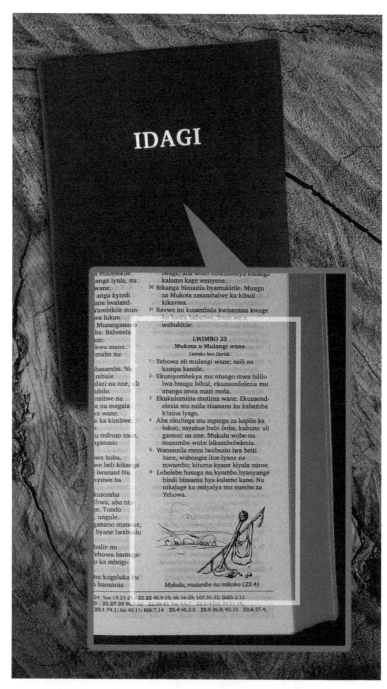

Bible translation work completed into their Kilega language
(showing Psalm 23).

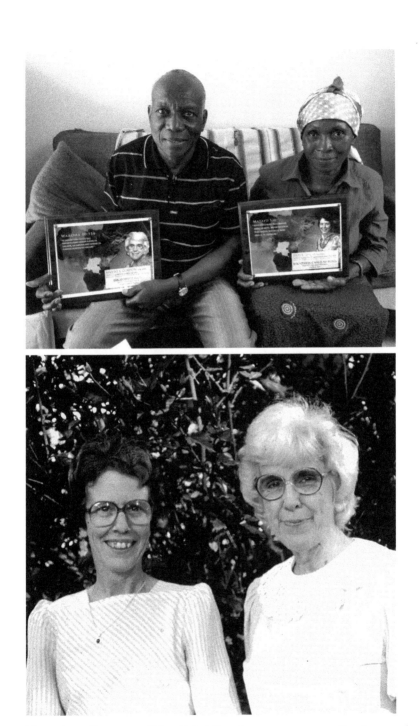

Bible Institute director and his wife holding plaques commemorating Joyce and Maxine's work; Joyce Owens and Maxine Gordon.

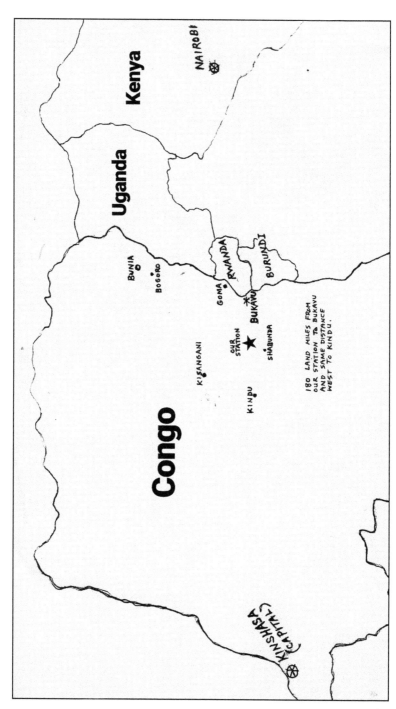

Map of their area in Africa.

CPSIA information can be obtained
at www.ICGtesting.com
Printed in the USA
BVHW022006160720
583764BV00019B/44/J